THE BLITZ

OPERATIONS MANUAL

AUTHOR'S DEDICATION
I dedicate this book to my father, Brian McNab (1929–2019), himself a survivor
of Blitz bombing, who died shortly before the publication of this book. A strong,
kind and generous man, and a loving father, forever missed.

First published in January 2020

A catalogue record for this book is available from the British Library.

ISBN 978 1 78521 640 4

Library of Congress control no. 2019908381

Published by Haynes Publishing,
Sparkford, Yeovil, Somerset, BA22 7JJ, UK.
Tel: 01963 440635
Int. tel: +44 1963 440635
Website: www.haynes.com

Haynes North America Inc.,
859 Lawrence Drive, Newbury Park,
California 91320, USA.

Printed in Malaysia.

All images are credited within the captions.

AUTHOR'S ACKNOWLEDGEMENTS
I would like to thank the generous help of two people in particular for giving me
access to their artefact collections for photographic purposes: John Thomas of
the 1940s Swansea Bay Museum (http://www.1940sswanseabay.co.uk/) and
Joseph Barrett (http://www.josephs-militaria-and-homefront-collection.co.uk/).
Thanks also go to Ted Nevill of AirSeaLand Photos for some excellent archive
photos, Lucy Doncaster for her careful editing and Joanne Rippin for her
ever-supportive project management.

▶ *An Observer Corps spotter takes up a precarious position on a rooftop in
London, with St Paul's Cathedral in the background. (NARA)*

THE BLITZ

OPERATIONS MANUAL

CHRIS McNAB

CONTENTS

Einen
Gruß
vom

Geſchwader

Auf daß
wir leben,
mußt Du
Hund
verrecken

Wen man lieb!
muß man beſchenken

INTRODUCTION

In the history of World War II (1939–45), indeed in all 20th-century history, the Blitz stands out as one of Britain's truly defining social, military and cultural events. Although the term is sometimes used loosely to denote all Luftwaffe raids over Britain during the war years, strictly it refers to the German strategic bombing campaign unleashed between September 1940 and May 1941, mostly under the cover of night. The consequences of this campaign for the island nation were profound – around 43,000 civilians dead, 139,000 injured, massive destruction upon Britain's industrial base, 250,000 homes completely destroyed and 2 million more badly damaged.

◄ *France, 1940. German bomber crews chalk up some appropriate messages on SC250 high-explosive bombs (the most common type of HE ordnance dropped during the Blitz) prior to a raid on the UK. (AirSeaLand Photos)*

The Blitz, when it began in earnest with a major raid on London on 7 September 1940, marked a clear shift in policy in the German air war against Britain. During the summer months of that year, the Luftwaffe's overarching strategic goal was to break the RAF in what we now call 'The Battle of Britain'. In this phase of the war, etched in public memory as sharp as the fighter contrails lacing blue summer skies, the Luftwaffe targeted ports, radar installations, airfields, aircraft manufacturing plants and, above all, the RAF's fighter wing, hoping to break Britain's aerial defences in preparation for a cross-Channel invasion, Operation *Sealion*. By early September, however, the RAF still appeared in defiant health and Hitler's psychological commitment to a British invasion was weakening, as his eyes turned east instead of west. There thus came a change of focus in a new directive, issued on 5 September 1940, calling for 'disruptive attacks on the

population and air defences of major British cities, including London, by day and night.' In effect, Hitler now intended to pound Britain's people and industry into submission. With this directive, and as the Battle of Britain slid into defeat, the Blitz was launched.

The attack on 7 September 1940, a daylight raid, saw 348 German bombers, escorted by 617 fighters, unload a lethal cargo of high explosive and incendiaries across the city of London. By 0600hrs, when the raid ended, much of the urban landscape was in flames, especially around the dockyard areas. Some 430 people had been killed and a further 1,600 injured. But this was only the beginning. Until mid-November, London was bombed almost every single night by an average of 200 bombers. (By switching to night raids, the Luftwaffe avoided the RAF's day fighters, and were faced with little more than ineffective anti-aircraft fire.)

Although London was to be by far the worst hit of all Britain's cities, over subsequent weeks the Blitz spread out across much of the UK, particularly from November 1940 and between February and May 1941. Cities targeted included

▼ *This view from the nose of a Heinkel He 111, flying at very low level (possibly for photo-reconnaissance purposes) shows fire engulfing the streets of London. (AirSeaLand Photos)*

Birmingham, Bristol, Avonmouth, Coventry, Southampton, Plymouth, Liverpool (the nation's second most bombed city), Cardiff, Swansea, Belfast, Clydeside, Hull, Sheffield, Leeds, Sunderland, Newcastle and Nottingham. The levels of destruction and death were profound, as were the changes in governance and daily life to which the people of Britain had to adjust. The entire society – men and women, children and adults – as we shall see, in effect had to mobilise if it were to survive, a process that Britain had fortuitously begun to implement in the 1930s. Thus millions of people found themselves in a plethora of new roles: fire-fighters, Air Raid Wardens, shelter marshals, ambulance drivers, rescuers, stretcher-bearers, first-aid parties, anti-aircraft gun and searchlight crews, evacuee handlers, and many, many more. Rarely has a society had to change its duties and its way of life so dramatically in such a short space of time.

The Blitz finally petered out in May 1941. By this time, the Luftwaffe was taking very heavy losses over British airspace, the product of seminal improvements in air defence, plus it was now building up to Hitler's great and ultimately disastrous adventure in the east, the invasion of the Soviet Union. Britain

▲ *An ARP warden passes in front of the wreckage of a bus parked between Arthur Street and King William Street, London, torn apart by an HE bomb. (AirSeaLand Photos)*

had not been beaten, despite suffering the casualties described above, and succumbing to further air raids (including the V-weapon onslaughts of 1944) later in the war.

This book is not about that history. Rather, it focuses closely on what the men and women of Britain were called upon to do to play their part in Air Raid Precautions (ARP) and Civil Defence during the Blitz months. Drawing on extensive collections of primary sources and eyewitness documents, it explores activities from the mundane to the profound, from how to black out a window through to surviving the detonation of a high explosive bomb. Reading the original manuals, what is striking is how the alien and terrifying – being bombed from above on a nightly basis – was turned into something that could be managed by society pulling together, albeit only just, and with many imperfections. Ultimately, it is a picture illustrating how exceptional ordinary people can be, when normality is not an option.

CHAPTER ONE

EVACUATION AND SHELTER

From the mid- to late 1930s, even prior to the onset of the war, the issue of effective shelter from bombing raids was a pressing task for the British government. The apocalyptic vision of a German strategic bombing campaign prompted the Home Office, along with various other authorities, to explore how best to ensure that the nation could survive such an onslaught, should it happen. There were two fundamental strategies advocated: dispersal and shelter.

◄ *Labelled like so much luggage, young evacuees are readied at a London railway station for evacuation. In three days alone in early September 1939, 1.5 million children were evacuated. (Getty)*

DISPERSAL

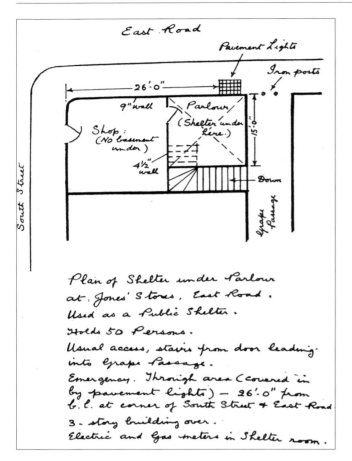

Plan of Shelter under Parlour at Jones' Stores, East Road. Used as a Public Shelter. Holds 50 Persons. Usual access, stairs from door leading into Grape Passage. Emergency. Through area (covered in by pavement lights) — 26'.0" from b.l. at corner of South Street + East Road. 3 - story building over. Electric and Gas meters in Shelter room.

The simple aim of dispersal was to shift people away from dangerous areas – typically urban zones with target-rich opportunities for the Luftwaffe – to safer places in rural districts or quiet provincial towns. The most visible face of the dispersal policy was the evacuation of children (see below), but there was also a considerable amount of 'private evacuation', whereby individuals or families chose to relocate to what were considered safer locations, often encouraged to do so by advertisements in local media. Some of the suggested locations were open to question. An advert with the headline 'Live in a Safer Zone' in the *Daily Express* on 2 September 1939 advertised new homes in a selection of areas that later received heavy bombing, including Dagenham, Wandsworth and Enfield. Regardless of whether or not the destination turned out to be safe, it is estimated that c. 2 million people moved home between June and September 1939. During the Blitz, there were also various 'assisted private' evacuation schemes for mothers, the women receiving some financial support for travel and those who billeted them taking a small allowance for their upkeep.

The other face of voluntary dispersal also came during the Blitz itself, when thousands of citizens in the worst-hit areas simply began tramping out of the cities in the late afternoon to find somewhere safe to sit out the night. 'Trekking', as this was known, was a ragged and unpredictable business, the columns of people appearing more as refugees in their own country. Londoners, for example, headed for areas such as Epping Forest, where they would spend the night in improvised shelters among the ancient trees, but also journeying to places as far away as Reading and Oxford. There, they would try to find someone to put them up for the night or longer (especially if their homes had been bombed); this was not always easy, as the legendary 'Blitz spirit' was not predictable or uniformly spread. Local authority billeting officers were given the power to force householders to take in evacuees, but they tended to shy away from using it – housing people in homes where the owners did not want them tended to lead to more problems than it solved.

EVACUATION OF CHILDREN

The policy of evacuating large numbers of children from cities to rural areas was a heart-rending exercise in familial separation, albeit one prompted by good intentions. The Government Evacuation Scheme had been developed in the summer of 1938

▼ *A shelter plan diagram for a 50-person public shelter beneath a convenience store, with notes provided by fire service personnel. (Author/Joseph's Militaria)*

◄ *Ramsgate's natural cave and tunnel systems provided hundreds of yards of basic but extremely secure air raid shelters. (AirSeaLand Photos).*

▲ *Emotional parents gather around a train about to depart from a London station, carrying hundreds of evacuees aboard for the journey to outside the city. (AirSeaLand Photos).*

by the Anderson Committee, headed by MP John Anderson, who that October became the Lord Privy Seal and the man in charge of Britain's air raid preparations. Having consulted with a multitude of authorities, including police, railway managers and senior teachers, a plan was developed for the evacuation of up to 5.5 million children and mothers with dependent children.

The evacuation plan divided the country into 'evacuation areas' and 'reception areas'. In the reception areas – the places that would receive the evacuees – appointed billeting officers were given the thankless task of allocating children to homes, the billets having already been surveyed, identified and recorded by members of the Women's Voluntary Services (WVS). In addition to being billeted in private homes, the children might also be destined for a number of large, purpose-built residential camps, built by the National Camps Corporation under the 1939 Camps Act.

The first major implementation of the evacuation policy began on 1 September 1939, two days before Prime Minister Neville Chamberlain announced to the nation that the UK was now at war with Germany. Note that evacuation was a voluntary scheme; parents were not legally obliged to send their children away, and the numbers of individuals evacuated

that September fell well short of the government's full list. Nevertheless, 1.5 million people were evacuated in a teary migration of humanity. They included:

- 827,000 school-age children
- 524,000 mothers and children under five years of age
- 13,000 pregnant women
- 70,000 disabled people

The evacuation process varied somewhat according to the time and place, but the following was typical:

1. Parents would receive an evacuation notice from the local authority, telling them about the date of evacuation, the meeting location (usually a school, as it was common for school classes to be evacuated as units) and what to bring. Parents would usually receive no information about the intended reception area.
2. Each child was to have a single packed suitcase or backpack containing essential clothing and personal items (see box overleaf), plus their gas mask in its container. It was recommended that the child's name should be written on the gas mask webbing. Luggage labels displaying the child's personal information and school were to be attached to both the child (worn on a cord around the neck) and the suitcase/backpack. Each child should also

have with them a packed lunch to sustain them throughout the day. The London County Council (LCC) recommended:

- *Packet of milk biscuits or similar*
- *Several small cheeses*
- *Packet of sweet biscuits*
- *Two bananas, packet plain chocolate*
- *Small unbreakable mug*
- *Please avoid greasy or sticky food, apples, oranges, and liquids.*

The same instructions also noted that, 'Eldest child in each family should take stamped addressed envelope and paper. They will write when settled. If too young letter will be written by one of staff.'

3. On the day of the evacuation, the parents took their children down to the school an hour before evacuation time, where they were handed over at the school gates to the teachers and members of women's volunteer organisations, who would be the guardians for the trip out to the evacuation area. The high emotion of this moment was sternly managed by stopping parents entering the school with their children; the school gates was the last place they would see their children for many months.
4. From the school, the children were moved to a bus or train station (or coaches would come directly to the school). There, they were loaded aboard the vehicles with their guardians and transported out to the reception areas.

▲ *Evacuees wait rather nervously for their transport. Note the white cloth gas mask bags hung around their necks plus identity labels. (AirSeaLand Photos)*

5. On arrival, billeting officers distributed the children among the designated homes and families. Sometimes this system might break down, resulting in unedifying spectacles such as the children being presented en masse in a school hall and gathered adults simply picking which child they would prefer to house. During the billeting process, it was not uncommon for siblings to be separated from one another, in emotional scenes.

Life for the evacuees was a perilously variable experience. Some remember it as a high time, a fortunate few ending up in opulent stately home surroundings surpassing anything they could have imagined. For the majority, though, it was an awkward and alienating time, housed with adults or families who, truth be told, simply didn't want a stranger living in their midst, even with financial recompense. (Households were paid 10s 6d per week for one child, and 8s 6d for each child if more than one was taken in.) Standards of behaviour, dress, speech and etiquette could be worlds apart when children from poor, working-class urban neighbourhoods were put amid middle-class families in decorous rural villages. Conversely, there were occasions when children from affluent backgrounds were located in homes of grinding rural poverty. At the darkest corner of the evacuation system, however, were instances of children placed with abusive and cruel adults, resulting in experiences that scarred many children psychologically for life.

The evacuation policy was not quite the success the government envisaged. The 'phoney war' of 1939–40 convinced many families that the threat was more imagined than real, and large numbers of evacuees steadily returned home. Even with the onset of the Blitz, the emotional wrench of separation seemed too great for many, and by the spring of 1941, 75 per cent of all evacuees were back with their families, despite the evident dangers. There would be further periods of evacuation in the UK, even as late as 1944 (during the German V-weapons campaign), but it never again hit the peak of those months in the autumn of 1939.

WHAT TO PACK FOR EVACUEES – GOVERNMENT LIST	

As preparation for evacuation, parents were instructed to pack a small suitcase for each child containing the following items at minimum:

Boys	Girls
2 vests	2 vests
2 pairs of underpants	2 liberty bodices (if worn)
2 night-shirts/pairs of pyjamas	2 pairs of knickers
2 pairs of socks	2 night-dresses or pairs of pyjamas
2 pairs of boots/shoes	2 pairs of socks/stockings
1 pair Wellington boots (if available)	2 pairs of shoes
1 warm coat/macintosh	1 pair of Wellington boots (if available)
1 pair trousers	1 warm coat/macintosh
1 pullover	1 warm dress or tunic and jersey
6 handkerchiefs	1 cardigan
1 toothbrush	6 handkerchiefs
1 face flannel	1 toothbrush
1 comb	1 face flannel
2 towels	1 comb
	2 towels

SHELTERS

The development of an implemented policy for sheltering UK citizens from air attack largely began with the Air Raid Precautions Act of December 1937, which directed local authorities to invest in the 'protection of persons and property from injury and damage in the event of hostile attacks from the air.' Despite the offer of substantial central government funding for this effort, there was much vagueness about this directive, not least because most people had little rational idea about bombing and its effects. In April 1938, Sir John Anderson attempted to focus the efforts somewhat. Two lines of activity were identified. First, Anderson wanted householders to take a measure of responsibility for their own protection, through compliance with official air raid information and the construction of personal shelter facilities in and around the home. Second, local authorities were to identify public or commercial buildings suitable for conversion to large-scale public shelters (or at least their underground portions), while also constructing new shelter facilities on public land, chiefly trench-type shelters (see below).

What emerged in reality was a rather haphazard and imperfect system of finding shelter for the public. Here, we will explore each of the main shelter types in turn, at the same time bringing out key points of public policy (or lack of it) in relation to taking cover.

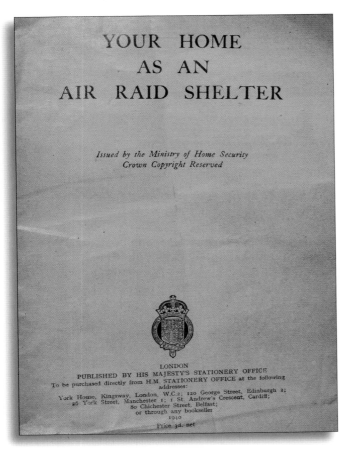

▲ *A reconstructed Anderson shelter. The corrugated steel shell provided only a structural frame; it offered little ballistic protection in itself. (Author/1940s Swansea Bay)*

THE REFUGE ROOM

The refuge room was any space within a home that offered maximum physical protection during an air raid, albeit requiring some measure of conversion and adaptation by the homeowner. Much of the thinking behind the refuge room was initially informed by the fear of gas attacks, but as the war progressed and that threat receded, the focus fell more upon creating a room capable of surviving high explosive (HE) and incendiary raids.

Some of the government instruction manuals, such as S. Evelyn Thomas' influential *ARP: A Concise, Fully Illustrated and Practical Guide for the Householder and Air-Raid Warden* manual, provided options of having a custom-made underground concrete refuge room, complete with 'air-lock, periscope [for viewing outside], gas filter and emergency exit'. He helpfully noted that 'the Cement and Concrete Association, London, [...] will supply, on request, complete particulars and plans of various concrete shelters.' Such lavish facilities, however, would only have been accessible to

◄ Your Home as an Air Raid Shelter *was published in 1940 by the Ministry of Home Security, one of an extensive list of defensive publications. (Author/Joseph's Militaria)*

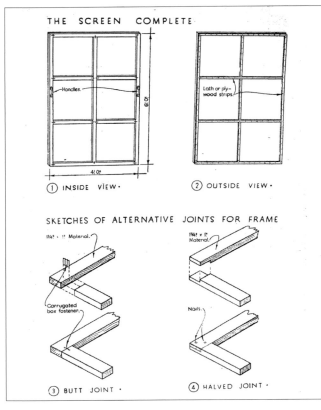

THE SCREEN COMPLETE

① INSIDE VIEW ·

— Handles.

② OUTSIDE VIEW ·

Lath or ply-wood strips.

4' 0"

SKETCHES OF ALTERNATIVE JOINTS FOR FRAME

1½" × 1" Material.

Corrugated box fastener.

③ BUTT JOINT ·

1½" × 1" Material.

Nails.

④ HALVED JOINT ·

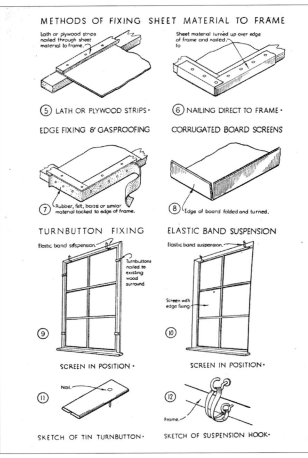

METHODS OF FIXING SHEET MATERIAL TO FRAME

Lath or plywood strips nailed through sheet material to frame.

⑤ LATH OR PLYWOOD STRIPS ·

Sheet material turned up over edge of frame and nailed. to

⑥ NAILING DIRECT TO FRAME ·

EDGE FIXING & GASPROOFING

Rubber, felt, baize or similar material tacked to edge of frame.

⑦

CORRUGATED BOARD SCREENS

Edge of board folded and turned.

⑧

TURNBUTTON FIXING

Elastic band suspension.

Turnbuttons nailed to existing wood surround

⑨

SCREEN IN POSITION ·

ELASTIC BAND SUSPENSION

Elastic band suspension.

Screen with edge fixing.

⑩

SCREEN IN POSITION ·

Nail.

⑪

SKETCH OF TIN TURNBUTTON ·

Frame.

⑫

SKETCH OF SUSPENSION HOOK ·

▶ *'Various kinds of window protection', from the* ARP *guide compiled by S. Evelyn Thomas. (Author)*

◀ *Government instructions for fitting lightweight screens to windows, which also provided a blackout measure. (Author/ Joseph's Militaria)*

Because of the perceived threat of gas, the refuge room had to be made air/gas tight, a job that required some DIY investment. Any fireplaces, openings, cracks or apertures (including pipework running into sinks or toilets) had to be sealed using materials such as wet paper, blankets, cloth and plasterboard. A blanket could be soaked in a mixture of salt water, soda, bicarbonate of soda or other alkaline solution to give it mild chemical-absorbing properties, then nailed or otherwise fitted across a window or door. Window frames were sealed with gummed paper. To make a gas-tight door, felt strips were affixed to all portions of the frame to make a tighter fit between frame and door, then a blanket was fitted over the door, nailed in place with wooden braces. The ambitious could even make an air-lock system using two doors, or even two hanging blankets that were at least 4ft apart, the gap in between providing a protective air space.

Other measures had to be taken to improve the refuge room's resistance to bomb blast. People were advised to

◀ *Recommended materials for window screening and blast protection included thick paper or cardboard, fabric sheets, and industrial adhesive films. (Author/Joseph's Militaria)*

▼ *The red arrows in this wartime illustration indicate the places in a room that would need to be sealed against gas leaks. (Author)*

◀ *A gas-proof door created by nailing a blanket around the door frame using strips of wood, leaving a partial opening so the door can still be used. (Author)*

▶ *Utilising books to create blast protection around windows and door. (Author/ Joseph's Militaria)*

stack up sandbags against the outside wall to cover any window openings; some publications even suggested bricking or boarding up windows entirely in the room. To guard against injuries from shattering glass, an interesting protective technique was to glue a light cloth, such as cheesecloth or curtain net, to the glass with flour paste; adding ¼oz of borax (sodium borate) to every 1 pint of flour paste would help guard against the growth of mildew on the cloth. A more sophisticated coating was celluloid sheets, glued on to the window with cellulose varnish; not only did this make the glass shatter-resistant, but it also allowed light to pass through into the room. Wire netting with a mesh not more than ½in square could be nailed across the window as an alternative means of protection.

TIMBER FRAMES AND MORRISON SHELTERS

The refuge room provided shelter from gas in particular, but from the start of the Blitz it quickly became apparent to

householders and the government that the real danger was from building collapse. In the cases where buildings folded in on themselves, either a refuge room itself might give way, crushing the occupants under tons of masonry, or the occupants might be entombed in a now subterranean space, surviving in a dark, dust-filled gap until the rescue services could hopefully detect them and dig them out.

The government provided instructions in several booklets and pamphlets about how to reinforce the refuge room to resist building collapse. A timber frame could be built inside the room, ideally along its centreline, whereby wooden upright posts held a timber brace against the ceiling, at a right angle to the ceiling joists above. To squeeze the brace tight up against the ceiling, the foot of each support sat upon angled

▼ *Recommended strategies of external blast proofing. The gravel fillings would absorb both blast and bomb fragments. (Author/Joseph's Militaria).*

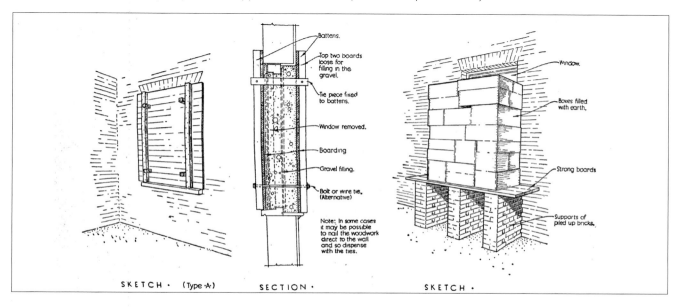

SKETCH · (Type ·A·)   SECTION ·   SKETCH ·

▲▲ *An illustration from the* ARP *manual showing 'Types of splinter-proof protection'. The volumes of earth required made such measures impractical for many. (Author)*

▲ *'Protecting the windows with sandbags'. If earth wasn't available to fill the bags, it was recommended that paper, ashes or other fibres could be substitutes. (Author)*

wooden wedges, which in turn sat upon a brace at floor level. By tapping the wedges inwards, the height of the frame could be raised to take the weight of the ceiling, although the installer was advised not to tighten the contact too much, which might risk damaging and weakening the ceiling. The Ministry of Home Security estimated that the timber for each

framework would cost anywhere from £1 to £4, the lower prices achieved by using salvaged timber.

Few householders went to the expense and trouble of building timber frameworks. Instead, when the bombs started falling they might simply sit under a particularly robust dining table, or shelter in the space under the stairs (structurally one of the most resilient features of a home). Mindful of these improvised measures, in January 1941 the 'Morrison shelter' (named after Herbert Morrison, the Home Secretary and Minister of Home Security) went into production as a more professional and dependable internal home shelter. The Morrison shelter was a metal structure, provided as a kit installation free of charge to residents of heavily bombed areas, if their annual income was less than £350. They could also be purchased privately for £7, only one application to the local authority being allowed per household. Not everyone was eligible to receive a Morrison shelter; they were mainly intended for those who lived in flats and apartments and did not have gardens, hence they could not build an Anderson shelter (see page 24).

The Morrison shelter was little more than a hefty steel cage, in which two adults and two small children could sit out a raid in packed proximity. It consisted of four corner uprights, a solid sheet-steel top (the government advisors emphasised the positive by pointing out that this surface could act as an additional table), a spring mattress forming the floor and wire mesh sides forming the four outer 'walls'. The mesh sides were strong enough to prevent crashing brickwork from striking the occupants, but they also hinged outwards to provide multi-point exits. Total dimensions were 6ft 6in long × 4ft wide × 2ft 9in high, and assembly was performed with steel bolts and a wrench and spanner (tools were supplied with the kit).

The Morrison shelter had a very 'last ditch' feel to it, and it would have taken strong nerves to hang on in there as the

▼ *A Morrison shelter in situ, complete with bedding for the occupants. More than 500,000 such shelters were produced and distributed. (AirSeaLand Photos)*

▼ *A woman affixes strips of tape across glass panels to prevent them shattering under the pressure of an explosion. (AirSeaLand Photos)*

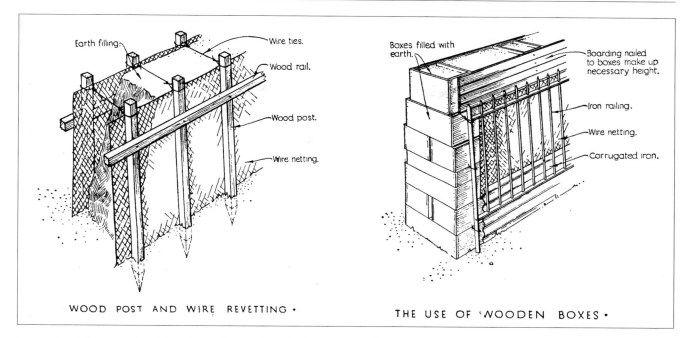

Earth filling.

Wire ties.

Wood rail.

Wood post.

Wire netting.

WOOD POST AND WIRE REVETTING •

Boxes filled with earth.

Boarding nailed to boxes make up necessary height.

Iron railing.

Wire netting.

Corrugated iron.

THE USE OF WOODEN BOXES •

house shook from nearby detonations. They actually had limited impact on sheltering during the Blitz period per se, as their distribution did not really kick into gear until March 1941, by which time the UK was entering the later stages of the night Blitz, although they remained a feature of many homes for the remainder of the war.

TRENCH SHELTERS

Building a refuge room or installing a Morrison shelter, while worthwhile, was nevertheless an activity swimming against the current of reality. The fact was that during an air raid it was far better to install yourself and your family in a shelter outside the domestic property, as the single-layer brick construction of most urban houses was ill-suited to resisting the blast effects of German HE bombs. For those with gardens, there were several recommended options for installing private shelters there.

Those with a true DIY mindset could follow government instructions for building a trench shelter. These were of varying degrees of sophistication, but the heart of the shelter was a trench dug into a flat and ideally dry portion of earth, the minimum depth of the trench ideally being 4ft 6in, meaning that the heads of the occupants, when seated inside the shelter, were below the lip of the trench. (It was recommended that the earth removed during the digging process be piled around the lip of the trench, thereby increasing the protective height through a form of parapet.) In terms of estimating trench size, six people could be accommodated in a trench 10ft × 4ft 6in × 6ft, and for each additional person an extra 18in of length had to be dug.

The trench had to be located at least 20ft away from the property 'to avoid danger from falling masonry if the house collapses'; thus this type of shelter was only really suited to those with big gardens, or several families with access to an area of rough ground. Given that shelterers might spend

▲ *These quite sophisticated blast screens would ideally be positioned just outside the home, to channel blast pressure away from the outer wall surfaces. (Author/Joseph's Militaria)*

up to 12 hours in the trench, damp was also a problem to be tackled. The *ARP* manual noted that 'gravelly ground is much more suitable than clay ground and will provide better drainage. [. . .] If the ground is clayey or damp, dig a sump (which can be emptied) and fill the bottom of the trench with about 6 to 10 ins. of cinders or clinkers, and, if you can, cover these over with duckboards. If water is struck when the trench has not yet reached its full depth, it is best to build banks of earth all around the top edges to the required depth.'

▼ *Workers labour to build a trench-type shelter in parkland. Such shelters were not popular, being especially prone to damp and flooding. (AirSeaLand Photos)*

▲ *This photo from* Your Home as an Air Raid Shelter *shows the way earth could be banked up and framed to protect external walls and windows. (Author/Joseph's Militaria)*

Given the earthquake effect of bombing, it was imperative that the trench shelter be resistant to collapse, otherwise occupying it could be more dangerous than being outdoors. The simplest way was to line the walls with a supporting material – e.g. wire mesh, wooden boards, corrugated iron or asbestos sheets (of course in those days the dangers of asbestos were unknown) – and then brace it with cross timbers. Even better was to line the trench with concrete, or use concrete supports.

The trench shelter was completed with overhead cover. This could be achieved with crosswise wooden planks supporting corrugated iron, galvanised or asbestos panels, the whole structure covered with a thick layer of earth (at least 6in) to protect against blast and to absorb flying splinters. Timber could weaken with damp, so 'Creosote or tar all timber, and see that the timber across the top is strong enough to hold the earth above it [even when wet]. See also that the roof slopes away to drain off rainwater.' Again, the more ambitious could create a concrete frame with overhead concrete roof supports. Whatever the design, it was important to create an entrance, typically top opening with a ladder and a hatchway, or at least a tarpaulin that could be rolled down and weighted in place when the shelter was occupied.

While the trench shelter was explained in detail in government manuals, shelter design was somewhat open to the ingenuity of the designer. Further options included cylindrical concrete bunkers partly sunk into the ground, capped with a concrete roof and packed around with sandbags, or long tubular shelters made from a mixture of concrete slabs, earth and corrugated iron. Some shelters might take advantage of natural features. In the author's own home, for example, a brick air raid shelter still sits at the bottom of the garden, dug directly into the steep, wooded hillside; in effect, the entire hill provides the top cover, while the dense woodland would soak up the splinters.

▼*Various methods of erecting window barricades. The carpentry and building skills required kept contractors busy in 1939 and 1940. (Author/Joseph's Militaria)*

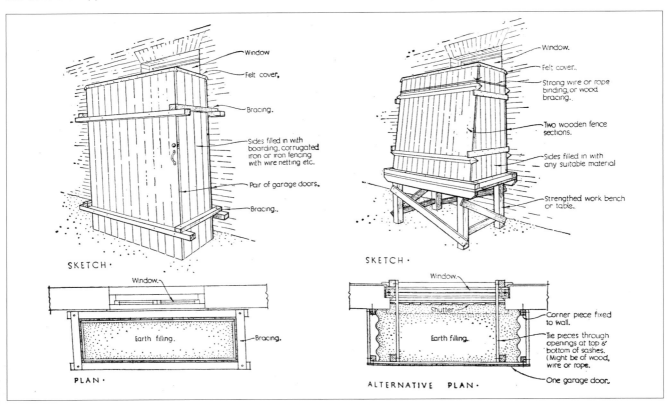

MATERIALS FOR CONSTRUCTING SHELTERS

The *ARP* manual gave the following guidance on the suitability of materials for constructing air raid shelters:

The degree of protection afforded by such shelters and dugouts depends on the thickness of the material of which they are made and on the depth to which they are sunk in the ground. The deeper they are the better. Surface or partly-sunk shelters of *reinforced* concrete are better than shelters made of ordinary concrete of the same thickness; concrete and sheet-iron or concrete and corrugated-iron are better than concrete alone; concrete is better than brickwork, but the latter is safer than ordinary earth or sand of the same thickness.

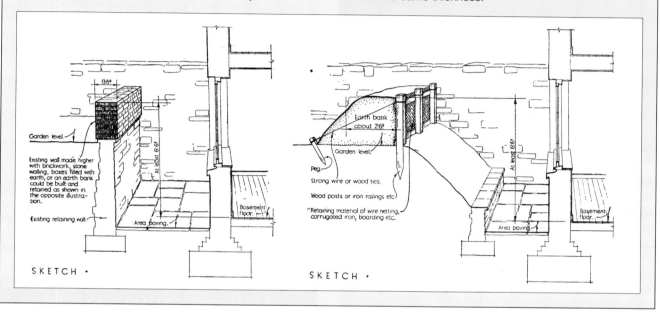

▲▼ *Illustrations from the manual* Air Raid Precautions in Factories and Business Premises. *The picture below demonstrates how to incorporate sleeping quarters in trench shelters built in company grounds. (Author/Joseph's Militaria)*

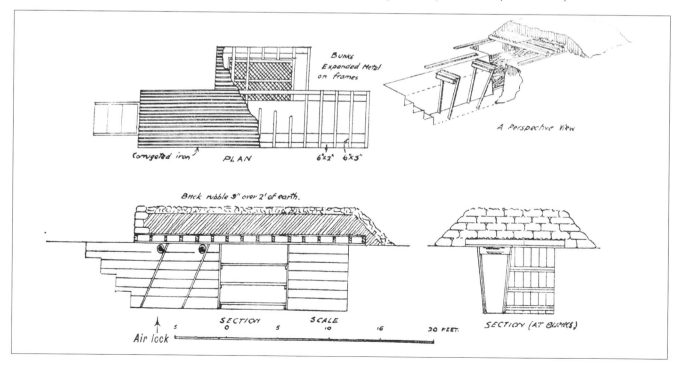

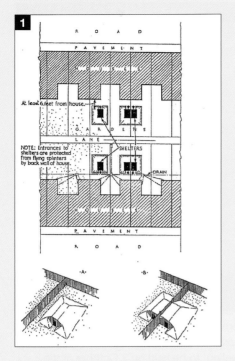

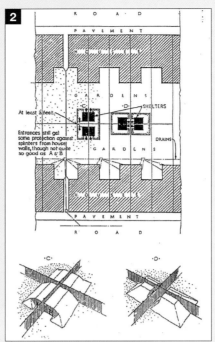

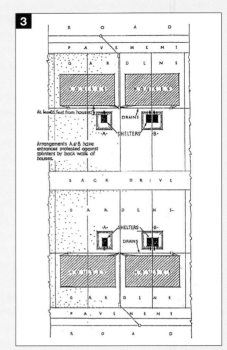

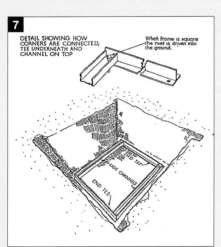

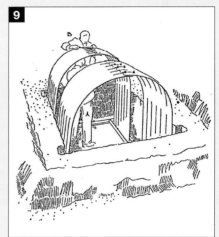

BUILD YOUR OWN SHELTER

The images here are taken from the 1939 Home Office manual *Air Raid Precautions: Directions for the Erection and Sinking of the Galvanised Corrugated Steel Shelter.* They show: 1–4) Recommended locations for the shelter; 5) The individual parts of the shelter in exploded view; 6) Pegging out and digging the hole to receive the shelter; 7) Arranging the shelter base frame in the hole; 8 and 9) Erecting the back and front arches of the shelter; 10) The correct bolting procedure for the arches; 11) Fitting internal supports and braces; 12) A view of the completed rear end of the shelter; 13) A view of the inside of the shelter, looking toward the entrance (note its height above floor level); 14) The completed front end of the shelter; 15) Covering the shelter with protective earth, to a depth of at least 15in; 16) The final shelter. Note the angled surfaces to aid blast deflection. (Author)

4
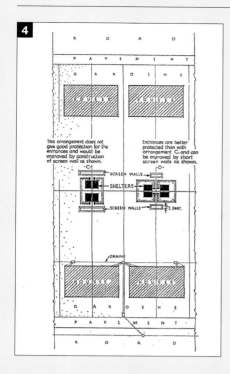

This arrangement does not give good protection for the entrances and would be improved by construction of screen wall as shown.

Entrances are better protected than with arrangement C, and can be improved by short screen walls as shown.

SCREEN WALLS

SHELTERS

SCREEN WALLS

2 feet.

DRAINS

5
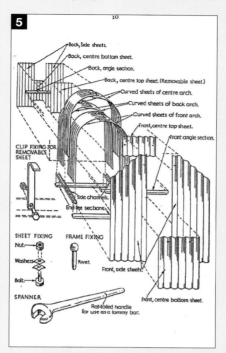

Back, side sheets.
Back, centre bottom sheet.
Back, angle section.
Back, centre top sheet. (Removable sheet)
Curved sheets of centre arch.
Curved sheets of back arch.
Curved sheets of front arch.
Front, centre top sheet.
Front angle section.

CLIP FIXING FOR REMOVABLE SHEET

Side channels.
End tee sections.

SHEET FIXING
Nut
Washers
Bolt

FRAME FIXING
Rivet.

SPANNER
Rat-tailed handle for use as a tommy bar.

Front, side sheets.
Front, centre bottom sheet.

6
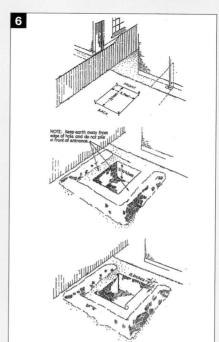

NOTE: Keep earth away from edge of hole and do not pile in front of entrance.

10
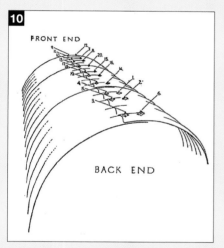

FRONT END

BACK END

11
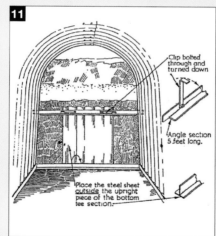

Clip bolted through and turned down

Angle section 5 feet long.

Place the steel sheet _outside_ the upright piece of the bottom tee section.

12
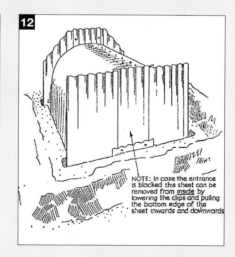

NOTE: In case the entrance is blocked this sheet can be removed from _inside_ by lowering the clips and pulling the bottom edge of the sheet inwards and downwards

14

ENTRANCE

15

At least 15 inches.

16
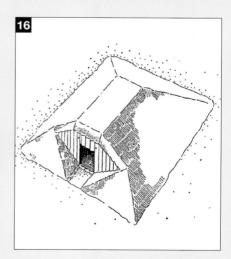

PUBLIC SHELTERS

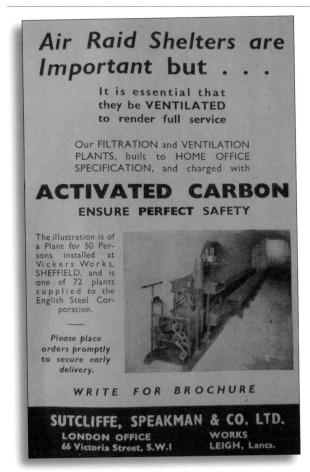

Air Raid Shelters are Important but . . .

It is essential that they be **VENTILATED** to render full service

Our FILTRATION and VENTILATION PLANTS, built to HOME OFFICE SPECIFICATION, and charged with

ACTIVATED CARBON
ENSURE **PERFECT** SAFETY

The illustration is of a Plant for 50 Persons installed at Vickers Works, SHEFFIELD, and is one of 72 plants supplied to the English Steel Corporation.

———

Please place orders promptly to secure early delivery.

WRITE FOR BROCHURE

SUTCLIFFE, SPEAKMAN & CO. LTD.
LONDON OFFICE
66 Victoria Street, S.W.I
WORKS
LEIGH, Lancs.

▲ *Adequate ventilation was a primary concern in shelter construction. Major shelters might install industrial ventilation systems, as seen here. (Author/1940s Swansea Bay)*

▼ *This Austin Reed gent's clothing shop has been adapted as a 24-hour public shelter, with sandbags providing blast protection and queue control. (AirSeaLand Photos)*

As we can gauge by the letter to the *Scotsman* on page 25, the subject of public shelters could be a hot one during the early months of the war, and indeed remained so to varying degrees throughout the Blitz. The Civil Defence Act of 1939 placed the responsibility for public sheltering squarely on the shoulders of local authorities. Part II of the Act stated:

2.–(1) Where it appears to the local authority that the whole or any part of a building is or can be made suitable–

(a) for use as a public air-raid shelter; or
(b) for use, in the event of hostile attack, by the local authority in carrying out any of their civil defence functions,

the local authority may post in the building or part a notice declaring that that building or part may be required for use for public purposes of civil defence.

This instruction to local authorities did not result in a plethora of public shelters by the time the war began. Collections of rooms and premises were identified, such as large basements in public or commercial properties, but they were neither entirely sufficient in number for local populations nor was it clear what adaptations were needed to make them acceptable for massed, regular public habitation. Sandbags packed around entrances and windows might be the limitation of modifications. Also, the owners of a commercial property could resist designation as a public shelter if they successfully argued that this imposition would affect necessary war production. As all manner of factories and business had been repurposed to war manufacture, this ruled out many buildings as shelters.

In addition to finding existing buildings as shelters, new ones could also be built, usually in areas of open ground situated in places thought to be less at risk. The quality of new-build shelters in many regions of the country could leave a lot to be desired. Worst of all were the above-ground brick shelters, essentially offering little more protection that staying in a domestic dwelling. In fact, the poor build quality of many of these shelters actually made them more dangerous than a home shelter. Eminent historian of the Blitz Juliet Gardiner explains in her work *The Blitz: The British Under Attack* how the official government instruction for such shelters stated that the bricks should be bonded with two parts lime to one part cement. Corner cutting, quick fixes and unscrupulous practices, however, resulted in sand often being substituted for the cement. The result was a horribly vulnerable building, apt to collapse with gruesome results under the pressure of a nearby bomb blast. Gardiner notes that in the London area some 5,000 public shelters had been built with the potentially lethal cost-cutting brickwork, while in Bristol 4,000 were demolished or rebuilt for the same reasons.

PUBLIC TRENCHES

The pre-war focus on shelter precautions largely revolved around the distribution of Anderson shelters. Furthermore, from September 1938 many local authorities, acting upon government instructions, had also been at work digging large concrete-lined shelter trenches in green areas to serve as emergency refuges for those caught in a raid. The newspapers from late 1938 and 1939 are replete with either advertisements for trench-building services or with local authority tender notices for such services. An example, published in the *Western Daily Press* for the City and Council of Bristol in January 1939, requests tenders for 140,000 pre-cast concrete sections for lining air raid trenches, giving a suggestion of the intensity of the levels of production. Indeed, by October 1938 alone, a million feet of such trenches had been dug. Yet in these days when the nature of the bombing threat and its social effects were not fully understood, the trenches were not intended for long-term overnight habitation, rather for people to take emergency shelter when caught in a raid. During the Blitz, therefore, tens of thousands of people found themselves hunkering down in dreadfully tomb-like and insanity-inducing trenches, lacking the utilities and space required for a 12-hour occupation by frightened and uncomfortable people.

▼ *A schematic of a trench shelter system. As the note at the side indicates, the trenches would be zig-zagged, to dampen blast waves. (Author/Joseph's Militaria)*

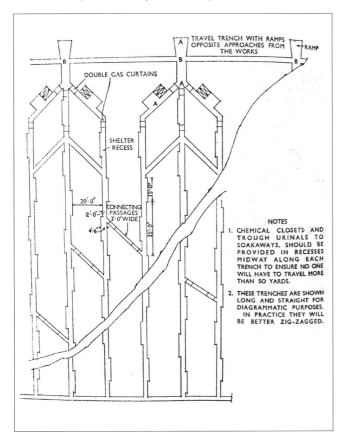

VARIETY OF PUBLIC SHELTERS – DOVER

Newspapers would publish lists of the locations of public shelters around the town, city or local area. The list published in the *Dover Express & East Kent News* on 24 May 1940 gives an indication of the diversity of forms these shelters could take. The list of shelters was divided into categories, and each shelter had beside it details of its location/address and the number of people it could hold.

The first category was 'CAVES' – the Dover and the Kent coastlines were well known for their superb cave network shelters, naturally occurring features that had been improved by local government development. Ramsgate in particular had 3 miles of tunnel shelters, complete with sanitation, electricity, lighting and even signposts to aid internal navigation. Total capacity was 60,000 people – considerably more than the area needed. The Dover newspaper lists 12 cave shelters, ranging from 75–1,400-person capacities, the largest being the 'Winchelsea to Priory Hill Tunnel'.

Next came the list of 'TRENCHES', six in total, with capacities of between 155 and 653. The longest element of the list is 'BASEMENT SHELTERS', mainly commercial properties. These included (with capacities): Leney's Mineral Water Factory (140), Fremlin's Brewery (314), the Scotch Wool Shop (68) and also the Wesleyan Methodist Church on London Road (125).

Next were listed four small (sub-100-person) 'SANDBAG SHELTERS' and four 'OTHER SHELTERS', two of which were railway arches. Finally came a reasonably long list of 'SCHOOL SHELTERS' with the note that they were 'Available for use by the public on Saturdays and Sundays, and on other week-days before 8.30 a.m. and after 4.30 p.m., and during school holidays only. *At other times they are exclusively reserved for the use of school children.*'

▼ *It was not only buildings that received bomb protection. This London bus has been fitted with anti-blast mesh over all of its windows. (AirSeaLand Photos)*

THE UNDERGROUND

Given the paucity or poor quality of above-ground shelters, it was understandable that many of London's citizens ventured down into the Underground stations when the raids were incoming. The combination of heavy concrete construction and subterranean locations meant that in many stations – especially deep-level lines such as Bakerloo, Central, Jubilee, Northern, Piccadilly, Victoria and Waterloo & City – the noise of even the most intense air raid above could be reduced to a distant rumble, accompanied by minor shaking. (Tube authorities recommended that sleepers on the platform did not rest their heads against the walls, which transmitted the vibrations of AA fire and bomb explosions.) As we shall see later in this book, the Underground stations were far from impervious to devastating hits, but they still offered a level of safety far greater than anything on the surface. Indeed, the government was concerned that people ensconced in the Underground might even develop a 'shelter mentality', and start to build strange, semi-permanent lives beneath London's streets.

At first, the authorities expressly resisted using the Underground stations as air raid shelters. Frank Pick, the chief executive officer and vice-chairman of the London Passenger Transport Board, with the support of much of the wider government, felt that the Underground must be preserved at all costs for the movements of essential war materials and workers, journeys that would be hampered by tens of thousands of shelterers crowding the platforms, stairs and escalators. (Trains ran until 10.30pm, often well beyond the start of an air raid.) But the tide of human desire for safety could not be held back, and within just a few weeks of the start of the Blitz some 175,000 people were sheltering within the tunnels. Unable to resist reality, the London Passenger Transport Board (LPTB) progressively started to make accommodations for the human influx.

From November 1940, metal bunks were installed on 76 stations, with 22,000 bunks fitted during the war (Moss 2014: 103). This was of course way below the number required, so most people brought their own bedding and improvised a bed on the platform. Chemical toilets and refreshment services were provided, the latter including six 'Refreshment Special' trains that pulled into stations well-stocked with tea and food. Many private and volunteer organisations set up booths selling or providing food and drink directly on the platforms. Ticketing for shelter was gradually introduced in many stations, not least to circumvent unscrupulous individuals who entered the stations early, earmarked a spot with clothing or objects, and then 'sold' the spot on to the fearful citizens later in the evening, for an excessive cost Sheltering in the London Underground thus became a highly organised affair.

To ensure that the tubes kept running for their intended purpose, the authorities implemented a system for allowing actual passengers to enter and exit the trains. Two white lines were

◄ *Typically, the track sections of the underground station were kept clear of shelterers to allow free movement of trains, although this station is obviously an exception. (AirSeaLand Photos).*

SHELTER TICKET SYSTEM

Once the LPT board had accepted the reality of using the Underground stations as air raid shelters, on 1 January 1941 they implemented a universal ticketing system to bring some order to the change in policy. (Note that some stations were already using ticketing systems by 1 January, and their example led the way for the roll-out through the whole Underground). Two types of ticket were issued:

1. Period Reservation Ticket

This ticket entitled the holder to 'reserved accommodation for night shelter'. The ticket was only valid for the station named upon it, and by showing this ticket the holder could enter that station and stay in it from 4.00pm until 'early morning' (likely shortly after the all-clear was sounded). The ticket came with the instruction that 'If you enter or leave the railway at any other station you must purchase a passenger ticket and pay the appropriate fare.' The Period Reservation Tickets were issued by the local authority in which the station was situated.

2. Casual Shelter Ticket

This ticket was issued on demand to those who had not reserved shelter accommodation in advance. After 4.00pm, such tickets were available directly from the station ticket office, but were provided only if there was space available, and the ticket was only valid at the station at which it was issued. On leaving the station at the end of a night's occupation, the shelterer had to give the ticket in on his or her way out.

Both tickets were free of charge.

---

painted on the platform. The outermost of the lines was 8ft back from the platform edge, and shelters had to stay behind this line until 7.30pm, after which time the passenger traffic on the tube would start to diminish. From 7.30pm, the shelterers were allowed to occupy space up to the second line, which was just 4ft from the edge. They were also allowed to occupy the stairwells and escalators (Gardiner 2010: n.p.). More details about the conditions and experience of life in shelters are given in Chapter 6.

The use of the London Underground for air raid shelters has become, via the photographic record, a visual symbol of the Blitz. We must refrain from over-romanticising the life of such shelters from safer times, however. For the people who found shelter here, it was rarely a comfortable or happy experience, rather one full of anxiety, discomfort and fear.

▼ *Flood gates on the Northern Line. Flooding from fractured water mains resulted in high death tolls. (AirSeaLand Photos)*

CHAPTER TWO

FIGHTING THE RAID

By the time that the Luftwaffe began the Blitz, in early September 1940, the RAF was already on the brink of winning the Battle of Britain. The aerial victory won by the RAF and Britain's other air defences in the day war against the Luftwaffe was rightly to be celebrated, a source of confidence for the nation. Yet the subsequent Blitz by night brought with it a new set of challenges, ones that would stretch the UK's defensive ingenuity.

◀ *ARP wardens and soldiers examine the wreck of a German Dornier Do 17, which crashed into Victoria station having been rammed by a Hurricane fighter flown by Ray Holmes of 504 Squadron. (AirSeal and Photos)*

EYES AND EARS

Britain had two key sources for detecting the approach of enemy aircraft: visual (line of sight) and sound direction tracking provided by the Observer Corps (from April 1941 the Royal Observer Corps) and radar-based tracking from Chain Home and Chain Home (Low) radar stations.

THE OBSERVER CORPS

The Observer Corps (OC) was a rudimentary but organised and vital nexus in British air defence. While British radar systems provided a highly advanced early warning technology (see page 38), its utility was confined to offshore tracking and detecting; as soon as German aircraft crossed over on to land, other methods had to be implemented. This is where the OC came in.

OC personnel were all volunteers for the roles, although many had previously been Police Special Constables who found themselves repurposed for war service, specifically for the identification, tracking and reporting of enemy aircraft movements. By the beginning of the conflict, there were an impressive 30,000 observers, usually identified by their steel helmets and their 'O.C.' armbands (blue-and-white-striped). They were located in Observation Posts (OPs) around coastlines, on the approaches to towns and cities, and in prominent and lofty inner-city positions, with good views of the skies.

The OPs themselves were often rather knocked-together affairs, especially in the early stages of the war, when they might be nothing more than a garden shed-type building located next to a telephone pole (to which the OP telephone was hooked up). Increasingly, however, the OPs became purpose-built brick or concrete structures, heavily sandbagged for additional protection. They usually had two storeys, the upper one featuring an open observation platform with clear views of the surrounding skies, the lower being for storage and administration. In September 1939, there were about 1,000 OPs around the country, and each was identified by a letter/number combination, such as A1, B2, C3, etc.

In April 1941, the Air Ministry issued a revised edition of the booklet entitled *Air Defence of Great Britain: Instruction for Observer Posts*. In its opening paragraph, it clearly stated the purpose of the OC and its sequence of aircraft reporting:

One of the first necessities in air defence is constant information on the number, course and height of hostile aircraft. In order to obtain this information, observer posts are organised over the whole country; these posts communicate their information by direct telephone lines to observer centres. The system further provides that the information shall be quickly passed from the observer centres to the various air defence commanders. It also provides the information needed for air raid warnings, but the issue of warnings is not an Observer Corps responsibility.

◀ *A spectacular firing of Z Battery rockets in low-light conditions. Engagement altitude was about 19,000ft (AirSeaLand Photos).*

SECTOR STATION OPERATIONS ROOM

At any one time, a typical Sector Station operations room was manned by about eight men plus ten women from the Women's Auxiliary Air Force (WAAF). The men were:

- Senior controller – Responsible for providing operational directions to the squadrons based at his sector.
- Assistant controller – Maintained communications with other squadrons outside the sector station area.
- Deputy controllers (2) – These men monitored communications with other sectors and also coordinated Air-Sea Rescue (ASR) efforts for downed pilots.
- Liaison officers (c. 4) – Maintained communications with OC Observer Centres and Anti-Aircraft Command. Also communicated with Group HQ Operations Room and the 'Ops B' individual responsible for scrambling pilots into action.

The WAAF personnel were principally used as plotters, working around a large general situation map table located beneath the male controllers and liaison officers. (The men sat on a balcony, so that they had a bird's-eye view of the action as it unfolded on the table.) The positions of enemy aircraft were indicated by coloured wooden blocks, each block bearing the name of the raid and its estimated

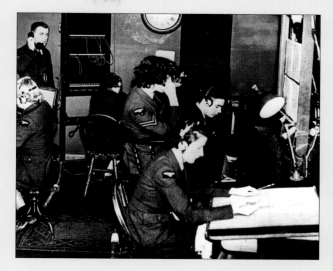

▲ RAF personnel process incoming information about a German bomber raid. (AirSeaLand Photos)

strength; an arrow placed behind the block indicated the direction of movement. The information on the blocks was refreshed regularly and the colour on a block corresponded to one of the colour segments on the operations room clock, giving an indication of the age of the plot in minutes.

▶ Using detail photo-reconnaissance images, Luftwaffe bomber pilots are briefed for an attack on the port city of Southampton. (AirSeaLand Photos)

▼ Two members of the Observer Corps in action. The man on the right is operating the Observer Instrument, while his colleague reports to the Corps Centre. (AirSeaLand Photos)

The Observer Centres referred to were locations where the multiple threads of OP information were coordinated and rationalised, before the information was then telephoned on to Fighter Command HQ at Bentley Prior (from where air raid warnings were ultimately distributed – see below), the Group HQ Operations Room and the Sector Station Operations Room.

OP EQUIPMENT

The *Instruction for Observer Posts* explained in detail how the OP was to be managed, and how the equipment therein was operated. Each OP had to be manned continuously by two men, although the usual OP team comprised three men, with one man at any time working in rotation. An appendix provided the list of essential equipment within the OP:

Item	Scale [number]
Telephone	1
Observer Instrument II. C.	1
Table (with celluloid)	1
Tripod legs	1 set
Tripod head	2
Canvas instrument cover	1
Canvas tripod cover	1
Tripod shoes	2
Spectacle case	1
Sunglasses	1
Binoculars with case and strap	1
Torches, cylindrical	2

Some items on the list require explanation. The key communications tool of the OP operators was the telephone. This was typically a hand-cranked magneto type – the operator had to wind an external handle several times,

charging an internal generator and providing enough power to make the call. Two specific types of phone were used (not just by the Observer Corps, but by many within the air defence network). The 'Telephone, Observer AD163' was robustly made, with high-quality woodwork and brass fittings. (There were also AD163B and AD163C versions, although the letters purely refer to the production batch, and not fundamental distinctions in design.) The AD1542 version is what has been referred to as a 'wartime economy phone', and this had simplified circuitry and cruder pine woodwork joined by nails, as opposed to the fine dovetail joints on the AD163. Both versions were connected to a 'head and breast set': the operator listened to the conversation through the headset ear pieces, and talked into a large, curved Bakelite microphone that was mounted on a chest plate. When the operator wanted to talk to someone nearby, without removing the microphone, he could simply swivel the mouthpiece to face away from him.

The binoculars were practically glued to the observer's eyes during periods of threat. The officially issued type were the Air Ministry 6e/293 pattern, which had a 6 × 30 magnification/objective lens diameter. Observers might also use binoculars of their own choosing; high-power naval types of binoculars (e.g. 10 × 50s) were particularly appreciated, as their magnification gave good visual acquisition over range while their wide field of view improved identification in low-light conditions. To ensure that the operator could use the binoculars and his naked vision in sunny conditions, the OP kit came with RAF Mk VIII Anti-Glare Sunglasses.

OBSERVER INSTRUMENT

The technical heart of the OP, however, was the Observer Instrument. This was an optical sighting device used to

◄ *Already becoming obsolete by 1940, sound locator devices could only give a rough impression of enemy bearing and distance. (AirSeaLand Photos)*

determine the location of enemy aircraft, once they were visually acquired. When an observer spotted an enemy aircraft or fleet, he first estimated the altitude of the aircraft as accurately as he could, or made a more scientific height calculation by triangulation with neighbouring OPs. The addition of the Micklethwait Height Corrector, named for its inventor, Eric Walter Eustace Micklethwait, to later models of the Observer Instrument introduced some mechanical precision into altitude calculations. Once height information had been acquired, the operator entered it into the instrument then pointed a mechanical indicator at the aircraft. This action moved an indicator on a small Ordnance Survey National Grid map and a pointer on the map indicated a grid location. It was this grid location and directional information that was telephoned to central control rooms. The observer centres had the advantage of reports from multiple OPs, as they were located in supporting distance of one another.

The problem was that during the night-time Blitz, the observers rarely had visual acquisition of the enemy aircraft, except on perhaps the brightest of moonlit nights. Therefore, from September 1940 Observer Corps detection activities often revolved around sound tracking. This involved utilising the Observer Instrument in a far less accurate way, using sound plotting (see feature box on the right). Angle measurements taken from sound, when reported from multiple posts, gave the plotters in the operations rooms enough information to calculate the altitude of the aircraft using the following formula:

altitude = angle × calculated distance ÷ 5

As an example of how this might work, if an aircraft was 6 miles from a post at an indicated angle of 20, the calculation would be:

20 × 6 ÷ 5 = 24 [24,000ft]

The Observer Instrument was mounted upon a tripod. Several versions of tripod were manufactured, either collapsible or non-collapsible, and of either all-metal or wood-and-metal construction. It was stored and transported in a canvas bag (listed in the equipment items). Yet many of the more established OPs had a fixed mounting position for the Observer Instrument, rather than a mobile one.

Despite their frequent reliance upon sensory information as much as equipment, the contribution of the OC was an important one during both the Battle of Britain and the Blitz, and indeed throughout the war. Radar technology had its limitations, and the aural and visual capabilities of the observer, allied to a bit of technology and basic mathematics, gave the British air defence some measure of fail-safe detection of enemy air activity.

▶ *Brick-built Observer Corps posts became more common by the Blitz years. Posts were often established on rooftops to give unimpeded fields of view. (AirSeaLand Photos)*

OBSERVER CORPS – SOUND SPOTTING TECHNIQUE USING THE OBSERVER INSTRUMENT

From *Instruction for Observer Posts* (1941)

(iv) **Reporting of Aircraft by Sound.–**
(a) Plots *must* be given of aircraft heard although they cannot be seen. The fact that plots thus obtained may be somewhat inaccurate is of no importance compared with the necessity of making a ready report to the centre, giving a 'sound' plot which shows the direction in which the aircraft is heard by the post.
(b) The method adopted is the use of a 'sound' circle of 5 miles radius marked in blue on the chart and labelled 'sound' circle. All sound plots other than the 'overhead' report are given on this circle. If the post is able to estimate by ear the direction from which the sound appears to come, No. I will set the pointer of the instrument on the sound circle and point the instrument in this direction.

No. 2 observer will then report a plot on the sound circle in this direction, whether the aircraft appears to be far or near, stressing the word 'heard,' e.g. 'plane heard, 3.30 at 10,000' (3.30 being the nearest half-hour by the clock code on the sound circle). The actual position of the aircraft, and, in time, its track, is worked out at the centre from the information given by plots from posts.

Therefore, the whole of the time that the plane is audible, reports at regular intervals must be given to the centre unless the plotter at the centre says they are not required. If the direction of sound remains the same, repetition of the same plot indicates to the centre that the plane is flying directly towards or away from the post reporting and this assists the centre in ascertaining the direction of flight.

RADAR SYSTEMS

Radar was *the* critical component of British air defence during World War II. Developed and installed during the 1930s, radar was Britain's early warning system, one that, when linked to fighter aircraft command-and-control networks, meant that the island nation could detect incoming enemy bombers well before they even left mainland European airspace. Not only that, but the radar signatures would yield crucial interception information such as speed, altitude, size of force and bearing.

The impact of radar was therefore profound. Most crucially, it enabled the fighter squadrons to scramble in response to an identified threat; they did not have to mount fuel-hungry, round-the-clock, on-station reconnaissance sorties, but rather only took to the skies when needed. Because ground control could vector the fighters directly on to the threat, full efficiency was maximised (there was little burning up of fuel searching for the enemy), giving the fighter pilots maximum time in the attack. (The Germans, by contrast, had only limited bombing and loiter time over the UK before they would have to turn for home.) Pilot fatigue was kept as limited as possible. Radar could also work both day and night, which meant that it had equal value during the Blitz as during the Luftwaffe's daytime operations. For those of the ground – Civil Defence and anti-aircraft gun crews – radar also meant that they had timely warnings of approaching raids, meaning that they could ready both themselves and the population to face the attack. Radar undoubtedly saved tens of thousands of British lives.

▼ *A Chain Home transmitter unit, which created the pulsed energy for the radar. (J.M. Briscoe/RAF Air Defence Radar Museum/CC BY-SA 3.0)*

CHAIN HOME SYSTEM

The centrepiece of the British radar air defence was the Chain Home (CH) radars, which proliferated across Britain as their value was increasingly proven and their technologies improved. At the beginning of the war there were just 18 CH stations dotted around the southern and eastern coastline of Britain; by 1945, there were more than 100.

The CH radar worked on a fundamentally simple principle. Radar transmitter towers 'floodlit' a defined portion of the sky with radio frequency pulsed energy. When the signals struck a sufficiently reflective object in the sky – specifically an enemy aircraft – a portion of the signal would be reflected back and could be picked up on a receiver and displayed electronically on a screen. The time it took between the emission of the transmission pulse and the detection of the aircraft 'echo' would give the aircraft's range, while the aircraft's X and Y coordinates could also be plotted, information then utilised to plot the aircraft's bearing. Through some complex calculations, the operators could also deduce a rough altitude.

A Chain Home station consisted of five core components: a transmitter and transmitter antennae array, a receiver antennae array and a receiver, and a receiver display unit. The transmitter was located in a small but well-protected building set amidst the transmitter antennae, which was the Type T.3026 transmitter designed by Metropolitan-Vickers, configured to operate at one of four frequencies between 20 and 55 MHz; the operator could switch between these frequencies in about 15 seconds. Hartley oscillators feeding a pair of tetrode amplifier valves gave the transmitter the ability to produce its short, frequent pulses of radio energy. The transmitter building actually contained two transmitters, one of them serving as a back-up device while the other was being used.

The transmitter directed its energy up to transmitter antennae, which were basically horizontal half-wave dipoles strung between four 360ft-high steel towers, these anchored at their outer ends to 600 ohm transmission cables that ran vertically through the outer towers.

The towers, which appeared very much like modern electricity pylons (although some CH systems replaced the towers with simple guy-stayed masts), were arranged in line facing the direction of the transmission; the multiple cables formed a shortwave curtain array with a front-facing broadcast pattern of about 100 degrees in arc (signals were weaker on the peripheries of the arc). It was best used facing out over water, and the signal experienced a wavelength change when it was used over land; it was for this reason that the CH network was a coastal one.

Return signals were picked up by the receiver array, which consisted of four 240ft towers arranged in a square pattern; these towers were made of wood, not steel, to avoid issues of interference with the transmission system. Each of the

▲ *A Chain Home transmitter antenna (one of four in the array), looking up at the cable suspension platforms. Each tower was 360ft tall. (AirSeaLand Photos).*

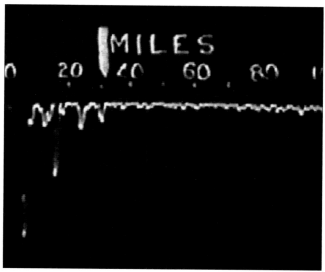

▲ *A Chain Home display showing several target blips between 15 and 30 miles distant from the station. (RAF Air Defence Radar Museum/ CC BY-SA 3.0)*

towers had two or three sets of receiver antennae set at various heights up the tower. The receiver itself, housed in a separate building, was a multiple-stage superheterodyne type built by A.C. Crosser, working to a Telecommunications Research Establishment (TRE) specification. The receiver passed the signal through amplification and filtering processes, which boosted the strength of the system and could be used to reduce signal interference. Finally, receiver

information was presented on a cathode-ray tube display, where it was analysed and interpreted by the operators.

The CH system was powerful and practical, with a range of more than 100 miles. It was limited, however, by the fact that it only really worked against enemy aircraft flying above 5,000ft; any aircraft making a low-level approach could fly to Britain relatively unseen. To counter this threat, in July 1939 a companion system was introduced, called Chain Home Low

▼ *A WAAF stares fixedly at a Chain Home screen. The knob on the left is the goniometer control with the 'sense' button to control antenna directionality. (AirSeaLand Photos)*

◢ *A 1940s visual representation of UK air defence, showing the flow of information between RAF Fighter Command HQ and frontline units. (Author)*

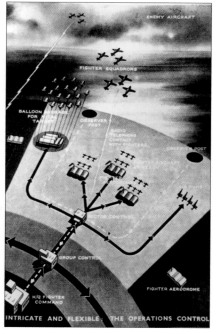

(CHL). The CHL radar had a transmission array consisting of 185ft-high towers, and the system could detect enemy aircraft flying as low as 500ft out to a range of 18 miles. CHL was also highly useful during the night Blitz, as it was better suited to vectoring night-fighters to within the maximum visual identification range of their pilots, which in darkness was about 1,000 yards.

CHAIN HOME OPERATIONS

The CH and CHL network was at the cutting edge of contemporary radar technology, but it would have been nothing without its operators. The majority of those operators were women of the Women's Auxiliary Air Force (WAAF), who found themselves working the most intense eight-hour days (often longer) performing the calculations and plotting needed to turn radar data into useful tactical information. For while the theory of radar detection at this time was perfectly scientific, the operators needed to be highly skilled and adaptive to deal with the ambiguity, interference and limitations of the systems.

In a typical set-up, a CH station would have an operator in the transmission hut and about eight people in the receiver hut, two to operate the receiver (operator and assistant) and six other people to convert the data into plotted coordinates on a map and to telephone that information to the Fighter Command Filter Room (see 'The Dowding System' feature box below). The big mental challenges of the plotting activity were making accurate placements of range and altitude, while defining and inputting necessary corrections; the process was later simplified somewhat by the introduction of a type of electromechanical analogue computer known as the 'Fruit Machine', which mechanically performed some of the key calculations and drove the plotter directly.

THE DOWDING SYSTEM

The 'Dowding System' refers to the informational network devised and implemented by Air Chief Marshal Hugh Dowding, commander of RAF Fighter Command, as a ground-interception system for detecting, tracking and responding to enemy air attacks on the UK. It was a hierarchical system in nature, starting with the electronic and human detection of an incoming raid and then cascading that information through various command and filtering processes until it reached the frontline British fighter squadrons, producing a 'scramble' command.

A key to understanding the Dowding System is that in 1940 RAF Fighter Command was divided up into four geographical groups, each group in turn divided into fighter sectors that contained the operational squadrons. The four group divisions were:

- 10 Group – South western England and South Wales (HQ: RAF Box, Wiltshire)

▼ *A Chain Home receiver room in operation. To the left is one of the two RF7 Receivers and on the right is the Mark 3 Console with the 'Fruit Machine' calculator. (AirSeaLand Photos)*

- 11 Group – South-eastern England and London (HQ: RAF Uxbridge, Middlesex)
- 12 Group – East Anglia, the Midlands, Mid Wales and North Wales (HQ: RAF Watnall, Nottinghamshire)
- 13 Group – Northern England and Scotland (HQ: RAF Newcastle, Newcastle-upon-Tyne)

Stages of the Dowding System

1. A German air raid is detected by British radar stations even as it forms up over France. The radar operators determine the raid's range and bearing and make informed estimates of strength and altitude. They report this information to the Filter Room at RAF Fighter Command HQ at RAF Bentley Priory.
2. The Filter Room personnel receive the radar data from multiple sources. They rationalise and process it until a clear picture is formed regarding the enemy raid, mapping the raid information on a large plotting table. This stage normally takes place within two minutes.
3. Via telephone, the Filter Room teller passes the information about the raid to the Operations Room in Fighter Command HQ and also to the relevant group and sector HQs (those towards which the raid is directed). Each of these HQs has their own Operations Room, where they also map the movement of the raid on a plotting table. The group controller decides which squadrons are best positioned to deal with the raid, and gives orders to sector HQ to scramble squadrons to intercept.
4. Once German aircraft are over the UK landmass, their progress is tracked by OC personnel in Observation Posts. They calculate the enemy aircrafts' position, altitude and direction and pass this information over to Observer Centres; those at the Centres then process this information and pass it over to the sector and group HQs, to give them the most accurate data about the raid in progress.

NIGHT-FIGHTERS

The Battle of Britain has virtually been defined in the British imagination by the silhouettes of the Supermarine Spitfire and Hawker Hurricane, the two primary fighters used against the Luftwaffe's daylight raids. During the Blitz, however, neither of these aircraft were ideally configured for the night-fighter role (although as we shall see, the Hurricane ultimately did play a role), so the weight of RAF air defence fell upon the shoulders of a very different group of specialised aircraft.

BRISTOL BLENHEIM

Night-fighters were commonly twin-engine medium bombers converted for the role; it was felt that single-engine aircraft did not have the size or power to take specialist night-fighter equipment, such as Radio Direction Finding (RDF) radar. (Later in the war, there would be several successful single-engine night-fighters in operation with the combatants.) At the start of the war, the main British night-fighter was the Bristol Blenheim, a rather lumbering aircraft with a maximum speed of 266mph – dispiritingly, the German bombers could often outperform the Blenheim – and five forward-firing Browning .303in machine guns. The night-fighter Blenheim was fitted with the AI Mk I radar (AI = Airborne Interception), with the transmitter antenna mounted in the nose and receiver antennae above and below the wings. The signals received from the radar were presented on a CRT display in the fuselage, where it was monitored by the radar operator.

The idea behind AI was that ground controllers would get the aircraft into the general vicinity of the enemy aircraft, then the AI system would pick up a signal and the onboard radar operator would direct the pilot to within visual range for engagement. In reality, the Mk I gave poor and confusing results. Supposedly 'improved' versions – the Mk II and Mk III

▲ *The Bristol Blenheim (here Mk 1 L6739) was better suited to night operations than day operations, although its poor top speed remained limiting. (Airwolfhound/CC BY-SA 2.0)*

– were installed experimentally on Blenheims, but they did not improve matters, all having unacceptable minimum ranges (the on-approach range at which the RDF equipment stopped working and the pilot had to transfer to visual acquisition).

BRISTOL BEAUFIGHTER

The big step forward in night-fighter interception was the marriage between an upgraded interception radar – the AI Mk IV – and a new and powerful aircraft, the Bristol Beaufighter,

▼ *A Beaufighter Mk II of No.255 Squadron at RAF Hibaldstow, in September 1941. Fitted with AI radar, the Beaufighter was the best British night-fighter. (Author/PD)*

which became operational just as the Blitz was beginning in September 1940. Powered by two 1,670hp Bristol Hercules VI piston engines, the Beaufighter had the speed (333mph) to catch and overtake the German bombers, plus an armament capable of ripping any German aircraft clean from the sky, no matter how well-armoured – it had four 20mm Hispano-Suiza cannon in the nose and six Browning .303in machine guns in the wings. The much-improved AI Mk IV, furthermore, had a genuinely useful range envelope: it could detect enemy aircraft out to about 3 miles and hold the signal until a minimum range of about 100ft. In fact, the new, low minimum range (previous versions had a minimum range of about 950ft at best) gave the problem that in poor weather the Beaufighter pilot might actually fly directly into the rear of the enemy aircraft. As the Beaufighter was not fitted with more powerful airbrakes, and sudden throttling down could produce engine failure, Beaufighter pilots often resorted to lowering their landing gear to slow them down.

AI MK IV INSTALLATIONS

The AI Mk IV went into several other British aircraft as the RAF expanded their night-fighter capability. There was the Boulton-Paul Defiant, a two-man single-engine day-fighter with a power-operated gun turret mounting four .303in machine guns. Heavy losses forced its withdrawal from daylight operations in the Battle of Britain and it was later used in the night-fighter role. The Defiant was not fitted with RDF, instead simply flying up into the dark battlespace and hoping to spot an enemy bomber trapped in a searchlight beam. With the AI Mk IV on board, the Defiant became one of the more successful British night-fighters, its performance in combat only second to that of the Beaufighter. The Hurricane Mk II was also used in the night-fighter role, and indeed later in the war received the AI Mk IV and subsequent models, although the bulk of its night-fighter work was mainly from 1941 onwards.

One oddity of the night-fighter arsenal was the Havoc I Turbinlite, a Douglas Havoc aircraft fitted with a 2,700 million candela searchlight in the nose. The searchlight was intended to search for and illuminate German bombers, but the steady improvement of RDF systems with the introduction the AI Mk IV rendered it obsolete. From mid-1942 the RAF began to use the de Havilland Mosquito as a night-fighter, equipped with new generations of RDF plus offering a speed and manoeuvrability that challenged even some single-seat fighters, although the development of this aircraft and its associated technology is beyond the chronological focus of this book.

GCI AND IFF

A leap forward in the night-fighter war against the German bombers was made in November 1940, with the introduction of the first Ground-controlled Interception (GCI) radar. This was actually a development of the CHL radar, but the RDF engineers sought to make a system that was far more accurate at plotting both friendly and enemy aircraft in the airspace, and in a real-time relationship that meant it was easier to vector night-fighter interceptions. The GCI operated on the 1.5m band, typically on 209 MHz.

◀ Ground crew arm up a Beaufighter. Note the AI Mk IV centimetric radar antenna visible in the Beaufighter's nose. (AirSeaLand Photos)

▶ *No 85 Squadron night-fighter pilots here wear dark glasses in the mess to preserve their night vision for later operations. (AirSeaLand Photos)*

GCI was important for introducing the rotating radar dish, which presented its results on a Plan Position Indicator (PPI) – the sweeping 'clockface' radar screen with which we are familiar today. Rotating speed for the radar dish was 0.5–8rpm. The GCI had a medium-range capability, detecting an aircraft at 500ft altitude at 10 miles distance and out to 90 miles for an aircraft flying at 20,000ft. Its great tactical advantage was that with GCI there could now be direct communication between the RDF teams and the British fighters; the radar operators could speak with the night-fighter pilots live via radio and guide them towards the target aircraft second-by-second, without the need to divert the information through various processing and command strata.

'Live' interception was also made possible by the development of Identification Friend or Foe (IFF) systems, which enabled ground controllers to distinguish on-screen between friendly and enemy aircraft. At the beginning of the war, two IFF systems were in use. The first was the 'pip-squeak' system, in which the aircraft's radio repeatedly sent out a 1 kHz tone, which was detected by ground-based high-frequency direction finding (HFDF, 'huff-duff') receivers. When the signal was picked up by three receivers, the aircraft's position could then be triangulated accurately. The other system was the first generations of active IFF transponders, which worked by receiving a signal from a ground station, and then emitting a slightly different signal in response. For radar operators, this meant that the friendly aircraft would be indicated differently on the radar display compared to enemy aircraft. The main IFF system aboard night-fighters during the 1940–41 Blitz was the Mk II.

▶ *A Ground Control of Interception (GCI) radar installation at RAF Sopley in Hampshire. The combination of GCI and AI radar dramatically improved kill rates. (AirSeaLand Photos)*

The introduction of new classes of night-fighter and RDF technologies, plus improvements in the training of night-fighter crews for the role, did result in a progressive upturn in the number of night 'kills'. In the first months of 1941 they were:

January – 3
February – 4
March – 22
April – 48
May – 96

From these figures, it was clear that by the end of the Blitz the Germans could no longer rely upon darkness to provide the measure of near invisibility it had enjoyed at the beginning of the war.

ANTI-AIRCRAFT DEFENCE

Anti-aircraft (AA) guns were the most thunderous and publicly audible British response to the German Blitz. During the very first days of the German night raids, the AA response was somewhat muted and cautious, the batteries waiting for accurate target information before letting loose a barrage. The problem was that such information was difficult to obtain (for reasons described below), and thus many Londoners expressed frustration at the apparent lack of AA response – during some raids, not a single gun was fired up into the sky. General Sir Frederick Pile was at this time the Commander-in-Chief of Anti-Aircraft Command. He was touched by the criticisms, stating: 'The intricate and enormous problems of night shooting were unknown to them [London's citizens], and impossible to explain. Londoners wanted to hear the guns shoot back; they wanted to feel that even if aircraft were not being brought down, at least the pilots were being made uncomfortable. It was abundantly apparent that every effort must be made to defend the Londoner more effectively, and to uphold his morale in so doing.'

▲ In 1942, offshore anti-aircraft defence towers, known as Maunsell Forts, were built in the Thames and Mersey estuaries. (AirSeaLand Photos)

AA COMMAND

Pile would also have been aware of the problems in underinvestment that AA Command had experienced during the 1930s and the first year of the war. AA Command had only been formed on 13 July 1938, under Lieutenant General Alan Francis Brooke. The new formation, although part of the Army, actually fell under the command umbrella of the Air Defence Great Britain (ADGB) organisation, headed by RAF Fighter Command. At the start of the war, AA Command had at its disposal seven divisions, but by the end of 1940 had expanded to 12 divisions, arranged under the following corps and regional structure:

- 1 AA Corps (1, 5, 6, 8 and 9 AA Divisions) – South
- 2 AA Corps (2, 4, 10 and 11 AA Divisions) – Midlands
- 3 AA Corps (3, 7 and 12 AA Divisions, and Orkney and Shetland Defences District Formation/OSDEF) – North

The expansion had stretched resources and personnel severely. A major shortage of AA weapons at the beginning of the war was plugged by inadequate purchases of Swedish Bofors guns and by repurposing old World War I artillery pieces and even machine guns. In terms of manpower, the AA guns were mainly manned by Territorial personnel, many of whom had received only basic training.

Nevertheless, the exigencies of war in 1939 and 1940 fuelled both the training and combat experience of the crews

◄ The QF 3.7in anti-aircraft gun was the most numerous of the heavy AA weapons deployed around Britain during the Blitz. (AirSeaLand Photos)

▶ *An ATS recruitment posted illustrates the close connection between the anti-aircraft defence and this women's service. ATS personnel performed almost every AA duty, apart from literally firing the gun. (PD)*

AA guns to send up heavy fire *without* accurate targeting information – the gunners would be shooting in what the military mockingly calls 'GDO' (General Direction Of). He gave this order both to improve the morale of the citizens the gunners were defending (which it did), but there was also a tactical reasoning: even if the shells didn't hit the enemy bombers, the explosions would at least disrupt their bombing runs, and therefore the accuracy of the bombing. (During a bombing run at this time, the pilots and bomb aimers needed the aircraft to maintain a straight and level bearing for at least 2 miles' distance; dodging the exploding flak interfered with this approach.) But technological advances came thick and fast, especially in the radar-direction of gunnery (see below), and by the end of the Blitz the shell-to-kill ratio had dropped to 4,000 shells fired to every kill. Thus AA Command's efforts did pay off in the long run.

GUN TYPES

For low- to medium-level AA fire, the British had the Swedish 40mm Bofors gun, licence built in the UK. The Bofors L/60, known to the British as the QF 40mm Mark III, was an auto-cannon firing at a cyclical rate of up to 120rpm, with a maximum firing range of 23,500ft. Although this range meant that it could reach the raid altitude of most German bombers during the Blitz, in reality the weapon's optical sighting system (although it did have a mechanical lead calculator) and the lightness of the shell meant that it was really only suited to aircraft within visual range. Thus during the Blitz, the Bofors took a secondary role to the heavy AA types, often being deployed around prominent military and government targets to defend against attackers coming in at lower altitudes.

The main AA weapon of the Blitz was the QF ('Quick-Firing') 3.7in gun. This artillery piece was the replacement for the earlier QF 3in 20 cwt gun, which had been the standard home defence AA weapon of World War I, and which was

and the numbers of modern AA weapons. Yet having honed its skills and procedures during the Battle of Britain, when they were engaging targets in daylight and often at low or medium altitudes, AA Command was then faced with fleets of high-altitude night bombers – an entirely different prospect.

KILL RATIOS

Statistically, on average only one German aircraft was destroyed for every 20,000 shells fired into the air in 1940. To put it another way, in September 1940, approximately 250,000 AA shells were let loose over London, but fewer than a dozen German aircraft were destroyed.

Part of the reason for the low shell-to-kill ratio was a considered decision by Pile in September 1940 to allow the

▼ *Captured German aircrew are led away by British military personnel, destined for a POW camp. Some shot-down bomber crews were lynched by civilians. (AirSeaLand Photos)*

▼ *With good symbolism for PR purposes, a British light anti-aircraft team man a captured MG15 machine gun, taken from a downed German bomber. (AirSeaLand Photos)*

QF 3.7in GUN – SPECIFICATIONS

Crew	7
Calibre	3.7in
Length	28ft 3in
Barrel length	15ft 5in
Width	7ft 10in
Height	8ft 2in
Weight	20,541lb
Breech mechanism	Horizontal sliding wedge
Recoil system	Hydro-pneumatic
Elevation	–5 to +80 degrees
Traverse	360 degrees
Muzzle velocity	Up to 2,670ft/sec for Mk I–III
Rate of fire	10–20rpm
Maximum firing range:	
Horizontal	3.5 miles
Slant	7.5 miles
Ceiling Mk I–II	30,000ft

used in small numbers during the Blitz, although mainly for airfield defence. The 3.7in gun was reliable, fast-firing (up to 20rpm) and had the requisite reach – up to 30,000ft – to engage the German aircraft properly. The shell of the gun weighed 28lb and was detonated by time fuse, the resulting explosion having a 45ft lethal radius.

Offering even heavier firepower than the 3.7in gun was the 4.5in anti-aircraft gun. This was actually an AA adaptation of the naval QF 4.5in gun. In fact, one of the reasons the QF 4.5in gun was turned into an AA weapon was that it was

▼ The muzzle flash of a 4.5in anti-aircraft gun illuminates the surrounding position; in the foreground we can see both rangefinder and predictor instruments. (AirSeaLand Photos)

intended to site the new gun around naval bases, and therefore the AA guns would have ready access to nearby stocks of naval shells. While the 3.7in gun could be placed on both static and mobile (wheeled) mounts, the 4.5in gun was only suited to a static turntable mount. One other key difference between the types was that the 4.5in gun was also sometimes fitted with a large mild-steel gun shield, which provided protection for the crew against bomb splinters. The 4.5in shells had a maximum effective ceiling of 44,000ft and a lethal radius of 60ft, although in balance the rate of fire was far lower – 8rpm – than the 3.7in gun, so the latter could send up a heavier weight of shell per minute.

FIRE CONTROL

As has been noted, night-time AA artillery was notoriously inaccurate. The problem the gunners faced was not just that of spotting the enemy aircraft in the night skies. Having seen the aircraft, the crew then had to calculate its altitude, speed and bearing, and then – rather like a shotgunner firing at crossing clays – launch the shell to intersect with the target in space, firing at where the aircraft *would be* rather than where it was (i.e. calculate 'lead'). This was a difficult matter, as the flight time of the shell to the target altitude might be in the region of 10 seconds, during which time the aircraft would have moved nearly 900 yards in distance.

The most basic, and quickly obsolete, fire-control device used by the AA crews was the sound locator. These were large instruments featuring multiple sound-gathering horns arranged on a moving mount, the sound collected via the horns fed into the operator's ears via a headset. The basic principle of the sound locator was that the operator kept altering the traverse and elevation of the horns in relation to the detected noise of an enemy aircraft; the point at which the noise reached maximum amplification provided the operator with a rough guide to the aircraft's height and direction, and this information could be passed to the gun crews. Acoustic location was, however, notoriously inaccurate, affected by everything from atmospherics to the psychology of the operator. Furthermore, during the Blitz the sheer number of attacking aircraft overwhelmed the locators, producing too many noise signatures for focused attention. As radar detection became more common from the late 1930s, the sound locators were progressively phased out.

At a typical heavy AA gun sight, there were three main instruments of fire control:

Telescopic Identification (T.I.) – This was a gun-sighting and range-finding instrument, with an eyepiece at each end of a bar and a prismatic binocular viewfinder in the centre, the whole instrument mounted upon a tripod. Two operators would turn and elevate the device until they could see the enemy aircraft, and the instrument readings would provide range and bearing information, which was communicated to the height and range-finder team (see below) for a more precise fire solution. The T.I. was also useful for getting a sharper view on the aircraft for identification purposes; the

ATS personnel who usually manned these instruments (indeed all AA fire-control instruments) received extensive training in aircraft identification, as at night all they might have to go on was a hazy silhouette.

Height and range-finder – This instrument was a coincidence range-finder, in which two images of the same object, gathered via lenses at opposite ends of a long tube, were brought into unified focus by the operator looking through a single (or sometimes stereoscopic) eyepiece. The act of adjusting the images to a point of focus provided, through geometrical principles, an accurate reading of range and height, information that was then fed automatically to the predictor. The most common types of height and range-finders were the UB7 and larger models by Barr & Stroud.

Predictor – The predictor was a large analogue computer device used to calculate the lead picture and shell time setting of the gun. Produced in versions by both Sperry and Vickers (at least for heavy AA work), the predictor was an energy-intensive piece of equipment to use, with up to six personnel gathered around it, operating its various controls. The information from the predictor was passed to the gun team, who would then set the shell fuse, lay the gun and fire it. One height-finder and predictor would normally provide information to an entire half-battery of guns (four guns).

▲ *Two members of the ATS man a Mk III prismatic telescope, used to spot enemy aircraft. They wear dark glasses to avoid eyestrain. (Getty/Fox Photos/Stringer)*

▼ *The No. 1 Mk III AA predictor, used with the QF 3.7in gun, was an analogue computer used to plot aircraft movements and calculate the firing picture. (NJR/ZA/CC BY-SA 3.0)*

Although this process sounds long-winded in description, it could actually be performed from start to finish in a matter of mere seconds by a trained crew.

GUN LAYING RADARS

The instruments described above naturally had significant limitations in night-time conditions, as they relied upon visual acquisition of the enemy aircraft. Yet by the time of the Blitz, AA Command was also entering the early, imperfect stages of radar-controlled gun laying. The first of these systems was the Gun Laying Radar Mk I, which had been introduced in late 1939. The system was based upon CH principles, with separate receiver and 20KW transmission centres, albeit on a smaller scale than the massive CH devices. The transmitter and receiver antennae were mounted on separate wheeled wooden huts, the huts set atop bearing plates on gun carriages, so that they were both portable and could rotate to track targets. By the beginning of the war the GL Mk I had an accuracy of 25 yards, which was within the lethal radius of heavy AA shells, but it was only able to provide slant range, but not bearing or elevation – a problem that when combined with some of the physical impracticalities in its use made it highly ineffective for night-firing.

The breakthrough came in early 1941, as a stop-gap measure while the improved Mk II was being developed. The Gun Laying/Elevation Finder (GL/EF), also known as the

▼ *ATS members cluster around a Sperry predictor system, which fed height, range and lead information automatically to the guns. (AirSeaLand Photos)*

'Bedford Attachment' (after its designer, Leslie Bedford), introduced both elevation and bearing capabilities. When the system was placed on a large area of chicken-wire matting (to reduce electrical interference from the ground), the Mk I and Mk I* (the latter incorporated some engineering improvements and anti-jamming technology) with the GL/EF brought about a major change in night gunnery, the radar communicating with the predictor and dramatically increasing accuracy – it was this technology that was largely responsible for the much improved 4,000-to-1 shell-to-kill ratios noted above. The GL Mk II version, which steadily replaced the Mk I between early 1941 and mid-1942, brought even further improvements, with greater range and accuracy, making the night skies an ever more hostile place for German raiders.

SPECIALIST WEAPONS

In addition to conventional AA guns and night-fighters, there were some more creative solutions to interdicting the Luftwaffe during the Blitz, although the out-of-the-box thinking didn't necessarily pay off in concrete results.

One fiery innovation was known as Z Battery, a short–medium range AA rocket system that launched ripple salvoes of 7in Unrotated Projectiles (UPs), so called because they had no spin stabilisation. The UPs were actually a Royal Navy development, intended for shipboard air defence, but by June 1940 Winston Churchill was backing their adaptation for land purposes. (Churchill was familiar with the UPs from his time as First Lord of the Admiralty.) Each rocket carried a 22lb HE warhead, which was carried up to a maximum altitude of 19,000ft, the warhead exploding either through a time fuse or a photoelectric proximity fuse. The idea behind the UPs was simple: once German bombers had been detected, salvoes of the rockets would be launched directly into the aircrafts' flight path, blanketing the sky with a spread of HE.

At first, the Z Batteries were composed of single-rocket launchers, as the Projector, 3-inch, Mark 1, but thereafter came the Projector, 3-inch, No. 2, Mk 1, which fired two rockets, and the No. 4 Mk 1 and Mk, 2 which could fire 36 rockets in a ripple salvo. Eventually the batteries reached the stage of firing no fewer than 128 rockets at once.

Z Batteries were at first manned by the Royal Artillery and the RAF Regiment, although from early 1942 operational control was increasingly passed to the Home Guard. Although impressive in appearance, the UPs were less so in terms of kills. Isolated kills were made, but on the whole the inaccuracy and long reload time meant that they achieved little. In fact, they tend to be remembered more for the panic they caused at Bethnal Green Underground station in East London on 3 March 1943, when their nearby firing caused a stampede among a large mass of people queuing down into the tube as an air raid shelter. The resulting crush on a stairwell caused 173 people to be killed and 90 to be injured.

Another interesting air defence innovation was the Long Aerial Mine (LAM). This was an air-deployed device, consisting of a 14lb bomb (8lb explosive charge) suspended, when dropped by a Handley Page Harrow bomber, by a small

▼ *The crew of a mobile Z Battery rocket launcher ready the weapon for firing. This No. 4 Mk 1 launcher could fire 36 rockets in a ripple sequence. (AirSeaLand Photos)*

▶ *This Z Battery launcher is the single-shot Projector, 3-inch, Mark 1. Firing 'unrotated' projectiles, the Z Batteries offered little in the way of accuracy. (AirSeaLand Photos)*

parachute that retarded its descent. Once the weapon had deployed, a 2,000ft length of piano wire hung from the base of the bomb, and at the end of this was a furled towing parachute, its weight keeping the piano wire taut. The principle behind the bomb was that an enemy aircraft would fly into the piano wire, the impact of which would disconnect the bomb from its main parachute housing, but at the same time deploy a miniature stabilising parachute set on the top of the bomb. Simultaneously, the towing parachute opened, which created heavy drag, dragging the bomb at the other end of the wire downwards and on to the bomber; the bomb would detonate on impact.

A total of 120 of the LAMs were held in each Harrow bomber, the aim being to create a deep defensive curtain through which the German bombers would have to fly even before reaching the coast. LAM operations ran from December 1940 until November 1941, and although a few kills were recorded, the small level of victories compared to the major effort of production and deployment meant that the project was eventually cancelled.

BATTERIES AND TACTICS

Heavy AA guns were typically sited in four-gun troops, each troop usually located on a predicted or common enemy flight path, or around particularly important targets. Certain territories were designated as a Gun Defended Area (GDA), headed by an Anti-Aircraft Defence Commander (AADC), and each gun position was controlled by Gun Operations Rooms (GORs).

The aim of the AADCs was to site their weapons so that they could subject the enemy aircraft to concentrated fire for as long as possible, and ideally do so during the enemy's bomb run phase. When protecting a specific target, such as a factory, four gun troops would be positioned in a square pattern, with the factory at its centre. Thus located, the guns could impose a protective AA circle that had about a 6.5-mile range from the factory's position.

BARRAGE TYPE

When engaging the enemy aircraft, the gun teams had several options regarding the type of fire they could put into the air, ideally maximising both volume and accuracy. When the gunners had poor target information, such as during adverse weather or technical difficulties with GL systems, the most rudimentary type of AA fire was the box barrage. In this case, the guns simply fired blindly into a 'box' of sky above the target area, hoping to make an occasional hit or at least to disrupt the enemy flight paths. A slightly better option was predicted concentration fire, which was generally used when the gun crews only had GL radar information, but not visual

▲ *ATS women use a Kine-Theodolite, a device used to record AA explosions on film to check the accuracy of the firing. (IWM/Getty)*

contact on the target. Here the gunners would establish a fixed point in the sky through which the enemy aircraft were predicted to fly, and fire a short barrage at that point. After they had done so, they would then switch to another firing point further ahead, and so on. The most effective of the barrage methods was continuously pointed fire, and was used when the gun crews had optimal information about the enemy aircraft, including visual line of sight (such as if the enemy aircraft were illuminated by searchlights). Here the guns maintained accurate fire that moved slowly with the pace of the aircraft, putting the enemy under heavy fire throughout the guns' ranges. If caught in such a barrage, the enemy air crews would experience constant rolling explosions within yards of their aircraft.

▼ *A plotting table is seen in the preserved No.11 Group Operations Room in the 'Battle of Britain Bunker' at RAF Uxbridge. (Danielstirland/CC)*

SEARCHLIGHTS

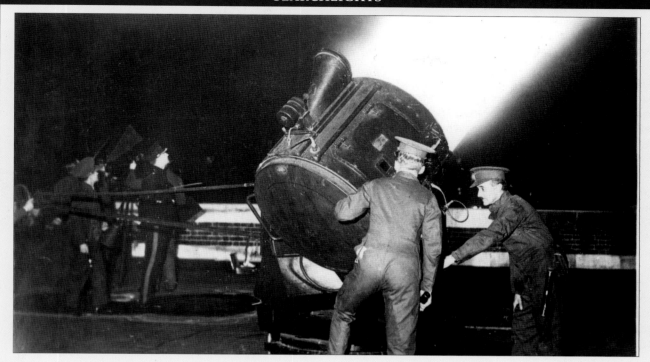

During the Blitz, the night skies above Britain's cities were split almost fantastically with dozens of shifting white light beams, issuing from searchlight batteries. The purpose of the searchlight teams was, ideally, to highlight an enemy aircraft or formation with its beam, and hold the aircraft trapped in the light while AA guns fired upon it. The ideal situation was for three searchlights to 'cone' an aircraft, making it almost impossible for the aircraft to escape through evasive manoeuvring. Searchlights also had utility in dazzling aircraft crew, thereby interfering with their formation flying or bomb aiming.

The most potent of the searchlight types during the Blitz was the 60in carbon arc type (150cm Searchlight Projector Mk 3), made by Sperry and General Electric, and replacing from late 1940 the less powerful 35.4in models. The 60in searchlight had a strength of 510 million candlepower, producing a beam length of 5.6 miles and an effective beam visibility of up to 35 miles. It was powered by a six-cylinder petrol engine, which charged a 15,000–16,700 watt DC generator.

A searchlight squad was typically made of seven personnel:

- searchlight commander
- azimuth controller
- elevation controller
- light operator
- generator operator
- lorry driver
- assistant

▲ *A 90cm anti-aircraft searchlight throws its beam skywards, while a sound-locator unit in the background provides the searchlight with some directional information. (AirSeaLand Photos)*

The control station for the searchlight was positioned some distance away from the searchlight itself; being close up to the searchlight would obscure the vision of the operators. The three men at the station were the commander and the azimuth and elevation controllers, who could operate the searchlight by remote control. In the early years of the war, the searchlight team might work in tandem with a sound locator team, but by the time of the Blitz they were more typically allied with gun-spotting teams or radar units. Target data would be sent electronically to meters on the station control mechanism, and the operators would then use hand cranks to make the correct adjustments to the light direction.

Another important innovation was the Searchlight Control, SLC, better known to its users by the nickname 'Elsie'. Introduced in early 1941, this was a VHF-band radar system directly attached to the searchlight itself, in the form of four receiver antennae and one transmission antenna. The radar system was operated by four operators in total, with three of them receiving information on range, azimuth and elevation via CRT displays. Elsie's value was that it enabled a searchlight crew to vector their light directly on to an enemy aircraft. This innovation, combined with others in RDF and night-fighter technology, was a contributing factor to the rising kill rates during the Blitz.

BARRAGE BALLOONS

They may appear distinctly odd to modern eyes, but barrage balloons did make a definite contribution to the air defence of Great Britain during the Blitz. At the height of the Blitz, some 1,400 LZ (Low Zone) barrage balloons were deployed around the UK, the majority of them around London. The purpose of these devices was not just to bring down German aircraft – although they were designed to do so – but also to create obstructions that affected the bombers' ability to make straight bomb runs, at least up to the 5,000ft maximum altitude of the balloon. In this they were successful, as areas that had heavy barrage balloon deployment were generally spared low-level attacks, which would have been more accurate.

The balloon itself was 62ft long and 25ft in diameter, kept aloft by a filling of hydrogen gas. It was anchored to the ground by a long steel cable that terminated in a cable drum. At both the lower and upper reaches of the cable there was a cutting link connected to a parachute bag. When an enemy aircraft flew into the cable, the cutting links would detach the cable from both the barrage balloon and the ground link, at the same time deploying the two parachutes from their bags. If all went to plan, the aircraft now had a cable snagged on its wing, retarded both above and below the axis of flight by two drogue parachutes. The parachutes were designed to impose six times more drag than the maximum power produced by the engines, thereby resulting in the German bomber stalling and dropping from the sky.

▲ Londoners gather around the Tower of London to watch a demonstration by a Balloon Barrage Squadron. Fewer than 30 German aircraft were actually downed in the war by barrage balloons. (AirSeaLand Photos)

◀ A vehicle-mounted RAF barrage balloon winch. Fordson trucks were used as platforms for a variety of British military vehicles. (Roland Turner/CC-BY-SA-2.0)

▶ A rather forlorn-looking barrage balloon sits ready for elevation on a street in London. Each balloon held 19,000 cubic feet of hydrogen gas. (Getty/Fox Photos/Stringer)

OBSCURATION AND DECEPTION

Britain's air defence measures during the Blitz included a range of tactics aimed not at destroying the enemy above, but at complicating their navigation and target identification. One basic device for achieving this goal was the smokescreen generator, dozens of which were transported around the country on the back of flatbed lorries. The generators worked by burning fog oil and vaporising water through an oil-burning furnace. When the water and oil mix was vented into the cold outer air it condensed into a heavy white smoke that clung to the ground. On occasion, the smoke generator was used to mask a specific target, such as a factory or military installation. Yet it was also applied to obscure features that the Germans would use to navigate to the target, such as reservoirs or rivers. (The smoke clung particularly effectively to the surface of waterways.)

While the smoke generators were an act of obscuration, there were also projects involving ambitious deception. The man behind these projects was Colonel Sir John Turner, former Royal Engineer but by World War II the Director of Works and Buildings at the Air Ministry in London. Turner was tasked with creating decoy ground installations that might lead the Luftwaffe away from genuine targets and cause them to bomb fake ones in less consequential locations. His first outputs were known as 'K sites', specifically dummy airfields complete with runways and models of aircraft, vehicles, storage sites and defensive positions. Sometimes real civilian aircraft would be used to add authenticity. Viewed up close,

▼ *The remains of a control bunker for a Starfish Site at Black Down in the Mendip Hills; no evidence of bomb damage has been found in the vicinity. (Rodw/PD-Self)*

everything looked undeniably fake and odd, but from high altitude and especially in low-light conditions, they appeared perfectly plausible. As an example of the optical illusions involved, sometimes aircraft hangars might be created simply by placing flat sheets on the ground, painted with the patterns characteristic of hangar roofs.

The K sites were primarily intended as daytime decoys. The 'Q' sites, however, were similar to the K sites but with various added lighting effects, such as fake searchlights, flarepaths, hangar lights and other illuminations, the purpose being to confuse German night raiders. Building on this principle, the 'QL' sites imitated not night-time airfields, but entire towns, including scaled-down models of streets, prominent buildings, factories, railway marshalling yards, railway crossings and other urban features, complete with lighting, subtly done as if the town were displaying numerous unintentional contraventions of the blackout regulations.

The most visionary expression of the decoy system was, however, the 'Starfish' sites. These were much like the 'QL' sites, but they featured various forms of fire-making and pyrotechnics to imitate a city under bombardment. As we note in Chapter 3, the German bombing raids often used to lead with incendiary attacks, the fires thus creating, in effect, marker lights for subsequent waves that tended to privilege HE bombs. The flames at the Starfish sites were created by various means. One technique was to have diesel or paraffin tanks set atop a frame about 20ft above a coal-burning fire; at the right moment, the fuel could be released, flashing up violently upon contact with the coals. A variation was the 'Starfish boiler'. This featured two cisterns – one of oil and one of water – the contents of which could be released together to flow into a heated trough containing a detonator system. The combination of water, oil and combustion produced flames that rose more than 30ft into the air.

Another incendiary mechanism was the 'Fire Basket'. Here, a wire basket featuring oil-soaked brushwood or reeds, plus a can of creosote, was set at elevation on an angle-iron basket base. A detonator system was placed in the base of the basket, and used to trigger the flammable contents when required.

Starfish and Q sites were typically set within 2 miles of an actual target area, and they proliferated during the Blitz and subsequent war years. In total, there were about 630 decoy sites of the various types built around the UK during the war, of which 230 were airfield and

◄ *Although undoubtedly spectacular on the launch, the Z Batteries made little significant contribution to the air defence of the UK. (AirSeaLand Photos)*

430 dummy towns, including 231 Starfish sites around 81 cities. The effectiveness of these decoys is hard to judge, as they were often within the circular error probable (CEP) of the highly inaccurate World War II German unguided bombs. However, the best data (from a 1946 survey) suggests that decoy towns were bombed on about 100 occasions, possibly attracting 5 per cent of the bombs intended for legitimate targets, and thereby potentially sparing an additional 5,500 British casualties.

The devastation unleashed upon Britain's towns and cities during the Blitz might seem to show that Britain's air defence measures had limited effect. This is not true, as the Luftwaffe lost some 2,265 aircraft and 3,363 aircrew between the summer of 1940 and May 1941. Britain was heavily bombed, certainly, but it was never a 'soft' target.

▼ *A board in a control centre provides details of status and position of anti-aircraft batteries around Swansea during the Blitz. (Author/1940s Swansea Bay)*

BATTERY	GUNS	STATUS	LOCATION	REMARKS
23	4	READY	TOWN HILL	
28	3	ENGAGED	MUMBLES	1 GUN U/S
42	4	READY	HAFOD	NEW SEARCHLIGHT LENS REQUIRED
56	4	STANDBY	KINGSDOCK	
58	2	ENGAGED	KILVEY	1 BARREL U/S 1 SIGHT U/S

DUTY ROSTA

▼ *This group level marker indicates that 25 enemy aircraft at 20,000ft altitude are being intercepted by 92 and 72 Squadrons of Biggin Hill. (Danielstirland/CC0 1.0)*

KNICKEBEIN SYSTEM

To aid their accurate navigation and bombing over the UK, the Luftwaffe bombers during the Blitz relied upon the *Knickebein* (Bent Leg) system of radar guidance. A radio transmitter in the occupied territories projected a radio signal, the centreline of which ran directly over the target. The German aircraft would follow this 'beam' to the target by auditory means; through a headset the pilot and navigator heard Morse dots if they flew to one side of the beam, and Morse dashes if they flew to the other, but when the tone was continuous it indicated that they were on the correct line. This transmitter provided bearing information, but not range guidance, so a second transmitter broadcast a further beam that crossed the other beam at the target, which for the bombers indicated a bomb-release point.

To counter the *Knickebein* system, technicians from the Telecommunications Research Establishment (TRE), based in Swanage, developed jamming transmitters code-named 'Asprins', which broadcast conflicting Morse dashes on the enemy frequencies. For the enemy pilot and navigators, this meant that the beam notes never resolved into the single tone. The jamming operations were conducted by No. 80 Wing commanded by Wing Commander Edward Addison, flying mainly Avro Ansons, which would make night patrols to detect the enemy beam frequencies and broadcast them to the transmitting unit. No. 80 Wing also conducted jamming operations against the Germans' later-improved beam system, known as *X-Geraet* (X-Device) and *Y-Geraet*.

CHAPTER THREE

SURVIVING THE RAID

Many civilians in the UK's blitzed cities faced the air raids in shelters, their biggest challenges being boredom, gnawing fear and chronic discomfort. Yet for those who remained above ground or in their own homes, or who sat in shelters in the worst-hit areas, they might have to fight more actively for their survival as fire and heavy explosive (HE) rained down from the skies above. As first-hand accounts attest, the civilians receiving the hammer blows of a German air raid often felt a wearing and agonising sense of helplessness. Their active response was typically limited to moving to shelter in decent time, a process that was fraught with all manner of temporal and physical challenges. Many people in those areas predictably and frequently hit (especially London in the autumn and winter of 1940) might begin their migration to public shelters in the late afternoon, regardless of any pronounced air raid status, to ensure that they found a place within. For thousands of others, however, it was the haunting wail of the air raid siren that would prompt their dash to a protected position.

▶ *The terrifying power of German HE bombs is evident here, in the aftermath of a bombing on Balham Underground station, the crater large enough to consume an entire double-decker bus. (AirSeaLand Photos)*

ALERTING THE PUBLIC

The air raid detection and defence process has already been covered in Chapter 1, yet once an impending raid was detected, it was incumbent upon RAF Fighter Command to transfer the information to the relevant civic and civilian authorities, and thereby initiate the air raid warning procedure. The UK had been divided into a total of 111 'warning districts', each of which had a control centre with a direct telephone line to Fighter Command.

AIR RAID WARNINGS

Transmitted via these telephones, there were three colour-coded stages to the warning procedure:

PRELIMINARY CAUTION:

Message: 'Air-raid message – Yellow'

This level of warning was given upon the detection of enemy aircraft approaching the UK, and was sent to control centres in the warning districts predicted as the targets for the raid. At this stage of the process, the message was kept confidential at the control centre, and not distributed to either the public or other control centres. Yet within the district, the information would be cascaded down through a variety of Civil Defence, police, military and fire organisations, plus industrial plants and governmental offices that needed to make special

▼ *Heinkel He 111 bombers unload their ordnance during a daytime raid. Eight aircraft could carry eight 250kg bombs in their internal bomb bay. (AirSeaLand Photos)*

preparations. Depending on the information available, the Yellow warning was typically distributed at about 22 minutes' enemy flying time to the target.

ACTION WARNING:

Message: 'Air-raid warning – Red'

The Red message was given when the enemy aircraft were just 12 minutes away from their target. Police units distributed throughout the target area, or other responsible Civil Defence personnel, were given the authorisation via telephone to sound the air raid sirens. These were the emphatic signal for the public to move quickly to shelters, whatever and wherever those might be.

RAIDERS PASSED:

Message: 'Air-raid message – Green'

This message, sent once again by Fighter Command, informed those at the control centres that the enemy aircraft had now left the district's airspace and no longer appeared to be a threat. This information was passed down to the siren operators, who now sounded the 'All-clear', which told the local populace that it was safe to come out of shelter.

Note: in cases where the *PRELIMINARY CAUTION* was issued to a district, but Fighter Command subsequently cancelled the threat, a *CANCEL CAUTION: Message: 'Air-raid message – White'* was issued. This was, like the *PRELIMINARY CAUTION*, kept confidential from the public.

▶ *An ARP warden's hand bell. Such bells were used to signal the 'all clear', and were used in shelters that were too deep for occupants to hear the air raid sirens outside. (Author/1940s Swansea Bay)*

AIR RAID SIRENS

The rather ghostly moan of the air raid siren became the Blitz's signature sound. The official instruction for the *ACTION WARNING* siren was:

A signal of two minutes' duration.
(a) A continuous note, rising and falling in pitch, the time taken from rise to rise being from two to five seconds.
(b) A succession of intermittent blasts of about five seconds' duration, with intervals of about three seconds between blasts.

For the *RAIDERS PASSED*, the 'All-clear' consisted of 'A continuous signal of two minutes' duration at a steady pitch.'

The most common of the sirens was the 10- or 12-port dual rotary type, manufactured by Carter (Nelson), Gents of Leicester and Castle Castings. These devices were, in the major towns and cities, usually powered by electric motors, although in rural areas less at risk hand-cranked versions were distributed. The sirens played across a minor third interval (B-flat and D-flat notes); the discordancy of this

▶ *An ARP warden in full gas protection demonstrates use of the gas rattle. Gas attacks were much feared, but were never used in the strategic air war. (AirSeaLand Photos)*

▼ *A Gents dual rotary Civil Defence (air raid) siren (museum display). The white plaque on it explains that the siren was originally sited at RAF Uxbridge. (Harrison49/CC BY-SA 3.0)*

City of Swansea
PUBLIC AIR RAID SHELTER

By requiring this shelter to be open to the public during Air Raids, the Swansea City Council has placed a heavy obligation on the occupiers, and it therefore appeals to the public to show its appreciation by protecting the property and interests of the occupiers in every possible way.

SHELTER REGULATIONS

1. Instructions given by the Shelter Wardens must be obeyed.
2. Animals must not be brought into this shelter.
3. Smoking is prohibited.
4. Any interference with the premises and the goods and equipment therein is prohibited.
5. Lighting must not be interfered with.
6. Unnecessary movement must be avoided.
7. On the "All Clear" signal being given, the public must leave the premises in a quiet and orderly manner.
8. Litter must not be left.

reaches of these rules should be reported to Shelter Warden.

▲ A wartime poster for the City of Swansea explains shelter regulations. Swansea was bombed heavily from 19 to 21 February 1941. (Author/1940s Swansea Bay)

▲ An ARP warden's gas rattle. The design was no different from that of a conventional football rattle, and one wonders about its audibility in the noisy chaos of a raid. (Author/1940s Swansea Bay)

musical interval enabled the sound to travel further, plus it struck an anxious psychological note. (Children naturally adopt a minor third oscillation when making a prolonged up–down–up pronunciation of the word 'mum', when pleading or in trouble; it is also the musical interval of the classic British 'nee–nah' emergency vehicle sirens.) The sirens were typically mounted in lofty positions, such as high poles or rooftops, to achieve maximum sound distribution.

MOVE TO SHELTERS

In theory, Britain's citizens went dutifully to the shelters when the *ACTION WARNING* sirens sounded and stayed there stoically until the 'All-clear' was broadcast. The reality was a far more patchy range of responses. Even in areas repeatedly attacked, there was a significant percentage of people who preferred to take their chances simply by staying in their own homes, even sleeping out the raid in their own beds. This could be a particular problem among the elderly, who sometimes had the fatalism that comes with age, but struggled to cope with the often cold and insanitary conditions in the shelters. Hundreds of thousands of people also had shelters either within the home (e.g. refuge rooms or Morrison shelters) or in the garden (Anderson shelters). These were precarious positions at best, and the occupants might suddenly find themselves having to leave the shelters because of threatening developments such as fire or impending building collapse.

There could also be a prolonged time of quiet inactivity between a raid apparently finishing and the 'All-clear' sounding, a period that tempted weary people to venture outside or back into their homes. This problem was widespread in provincial towns and areas that were on the enemy flight path to a major target, but were rarely, if ever, attacked themselves. My own father, Brian McNab, lived in Wakefield during the Blitz, a town where the population was frequently sent to the shelters – German bomber fleets would pass overhead or nearby, heading to Leeds, Sheffield or Manchester – but rarely touched by bombs, with a fatal exception. On the night of 14 March 1941, Brian, his sister Jean and his mother (his father was out on ARP duty) heard the warning siren and followed their usual procedure, heading next door to huddle with their neighbour, a Mrs Clegg, in her deep cellar. A complete lack of war sounds (no distant explosions or anti-aircraft fire), plus the cold and damp, led to the decision around 10.50pm to head upstairs for a cup of tea. It was at this moment that a single German Heinkel He 111 bomber, its navigation scrambled by British jamming, randomly released two SC 1000 1,000kg (2,200lb) HE bombs directly over the Thornes Road street in which the McNab family lived. Brian remembers:

She [Mrs Clegg] came out with the tea … and we were saying how it had all been very quiet tonight when we heard a slow drone in the sky. It was just a gentle hum. And we wondered whether we ought to go down into the cellar again, but nothing happened so we stayed put. Then as we were sat there the droning got nearer and nearer. We felt at this point that we should go back to the cellar, but we suddenly heard a whistle in the sky, getting louder and louder. It started off right in the distance but built to a crescendo … we seemed to be listening to this, absolutely transfixed, for ages. Then it seemed as if the heavens had opened, an unbelievable roar. The windows came out. The blast threw us all forward out of the sofa into the fireplace, then hurled us back while at the same time soot came rushing out of the chimney and covered us. I would have sworn that the bomb was on our house next door…

Although the McNab house had actually survived – just – numerous other homes had been completely wiped out. Moreover, six neighbours had been killed, most of the street having ignored the lack of 'All-clear' and behaved exactly as my father's family had.

The destruction rendered by just two bombs was astonishing. One house had completely vanished, while another was shorn in half at a 45-degree angle. Twin infants were discovered dead in their cots without a mark on them, killed by the blast alone. A female neighbour had been decapitated. The entire street was covered in a thick layer of soot, which had been sucked from the chimneys by the bombs' vacuum. It was a brutal introduction to the reality of war, even if it was on a scale far, far smaller than that experienced in many of the big towns and cities.

▼ *An unexploded bomb is detonated under controlled conditions at RAF Helmswell in late summer, 1940. (AirSeaLand Photos)*

FIRE AND EXPLOSIONS

The Thornes Road bombing consisted of just two isolated HE bombs, weighing a tonne each. Yet some major cities would receive hundreds of tons of ordnance, both HE and incendiary, for multiple nights in a row. In the manual *Air Raids: What you must know, what you must do!*, produced in 1940 and (updated) in 1941, the Ministry of Home Security attempted to educate the public about the dangers of German ordnance, and some basic safety principles to raise the prospect of safety. We will draw here on some of their insights, supplemented by additional information.

INCENDIARY BOMBS

As the Blitz progressed, German air raids tended to open not with the heavy hammer of HE bombs, but with the dropping of thousands of small incendiary devices. (The munition choice could of course vary with the target type.) The tactical objective of leading with incendiaries was to start destructive fires over the target area, weakening structures prior to dropping the wall-crushing HE bombs, and also to act as target markers or subsequent waves of aircraft. The widespread fires caused by the incendiaries also, in their own right, caused vast swathes of damage; these small bombs would lodge themselves in the roofs and upper floors of buildings, generating fearsome hissing blazes in locations that were difficult to reach for the fire crews.

The main incendiary type was the *Brandbomb 1 kg Elektron* or B1E. Measuring 343mm (13in 6in) in length and 51mm (2in) in diameter, and weighing just 1kg (2lb 3oz), the weapon consisted of a magnesium alloy outer body – itself highly combustible – with a thermite inner filling. Drop stabilisation was provided by a short steel tail with three fins. The fuse of the weapon was typically a simple percussion type that triggered the burning process, although some types were fitted with small explosive charges that blew open the burning casing after a seven-minute delay, throwing shrapnel and the flaming parts of the bomb out to a distance of around 32ft.

Incendiaries were dropped in very large numbers, using both fixed and droppable containers of various sizes. The government *Air Raids* manual clearly explained the effect of the incendiary on its target:

When the fire bomb strikes a hard surface such as a tiled roof, the impact operates a fuse which ignites the thermite core of the bomb. This burns at a very high temperature [up to 2,204°C/4,000°F] and quickly ignites the magnesium shell or casing, which then burns with intense heat. There is some spluttering for about a minute, during which burning metal may be thrown as far as 30 feet and will set fire to anything within reach. After this the bomb collapses into a small pool of molten metal

◄ *The 1kg incendiary bomb. Burning thermite would spit out of the holes around the nose, creating a further hazard for those attempting to clear the device. (Author/1940s Swansea Bay)*

▶ *A wartime British diagram showing the internal structure of the Elektron incendiary bomb. Note the impact fuse in the head. (Author/Joseph's Militaria)*

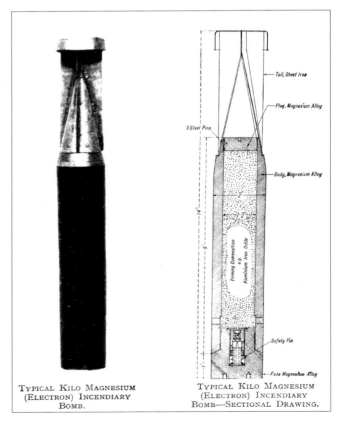

TYPICAL KILO MAGNESIUM (ELECTRON) INCENDIARY BOMB.

TYPICAL KILO MAGNESIUM (ELECTRON) INCENDIARY BOMB—SECTIONAL DRAWING.

which continues to burn with intense heat, but without spluttering, for about 10 minutes.

Multiple incendiaries burning within a property could gut the building with terrifying rapidity if they were not extinguished quickly. The Germans also worked on improved designs to enhance the destruction. For example, some incendiaries were fitted with hardened nose caps to enable them to penetrate through tile or slate roofs before ignition; this meant that they would burn within the building, and not expend much of their pyrotechnic effort on the outer shell.

During the Blitz, the Luftwaffe also dropped numbers of *Flam* or *Flammenbombe* weapons, known to the British as Oil Bombs. These weapons essentially took 250kg (550lb) and 500kg (1,100lb) bomb cases and replaced the HE content with flammable oil, a bursting charge igniting the oil and blowing open the casing upon impact. The Oil Bombs were, thankfully, unreliable weapons, the case often bursting open and simply spreading the gloopy contents over a wide area. When they did ignite, however, the resulting fire was voracious and over a wide area.

HOUSEHOLD FIRE-FIGHTING

Although fire-fighting was best handled by the professional fire services, the government provided instruction on how householders could tackle the threat themselves, *in extremis*. In fact, in a reversal of normal peacetime policy, the Home Office manual *The Protection of Your Home Against Air Raids* (1938) stated that the householder should attempt to extinguish a house fire themselves as the *first* line of response, and only if they could not do so should they contact the emergency services. The government also recommended that the householder implement all the anti-fire preparatory measures outlined in their recommendations, including having to hand sand/earth and water buckets, a stirrup pump, a fire hoe and a Redhill sand container (see below for more details).

Specifically for tackling incendiary bombs, it was later recommended that the householder have smothering devices at hand, specifically sandbags or sandmats. Sandbags were only to be half-filled to make them light enough to manage, and it was recommended that the corners be tied in knots so that they could be grasped more easily. A sandmat was manufactured from half a sandbag filled with about 15lb of dry sand, earth or soil, and then sewed up. The instructions stated that a sandmat should never exceed 20lb, as it became more difficult to handle beyond such a weight. By only partially filling the sandmat, the object could be lifted and placed with one hand (meaning you could keep your body further from the flames) and it could be gripped by the loose material on the top-centre; you did not want your fingers to protrude around the sides and lower edges of the sandmat, where they would be burnt by the intense heat of the flames below.

Fire not only came from incendiary bombs, but also from the fires started by HE munitions and from the embers, flames and heat of nearby conflagrations, or the jets of flame resulting from fractured and ignited gas mains.

▲ *A standard issue warden's fire bucket, used to hold either sand or gravel (to smother incendiaries) or water (for the stirrup pump). (Author/1940s Swansea Bay)*

▼ *A colour illustration in the* ARP *visualises an 'Incendiary bomb and its effects' in a typical British living room, the device having punched through the ceiling. (Author)*

HAND STIRRUP PUMP

The hand stirrup pump was a simple hand-operated water pump, produced in hundreds of thousands and sold or distributed to both Civil Defence emergency teams and to members of the general public. The device consisted of a metal suction and compression tube, operated by a large U-shaped handle and fitted with an outlet hose, plus a stabilising footrest on a projecting arm that gave the pump its 'stirrup' title. To operate the pump, one person placed the bottom of the pump into a bucket of water, the footrest sitting on the floor to the side of the bucket, the operator placing his or her foot and bodyweight on to it for stabilisation. The operator would now pump the handle up and down to draw water into the system and propel it out through the hose, which was handled by another individual. The spray itself could be projected out to a distance of 12–15ft, and a button on the dual-purpose nozzle could switch the water outflow between a strong, thick jet to a fine and soaking spray.

It was important that the householder keep the stirrup pump in a good state of repair. A spate of concerned newspaper stories from 1940 reveal that people would often test the pump on purchase, but then leave it unmaintained until an emergency, during which time components had rusted and malfunctions subsequently occurred. It was recommended that the owner grease metal components and also perform a routine test of the pump every three weeks.

▼ *A hand stirrup pump in its ready-to-use state; note how the 'stirrup' is placed, on the floor outside the bucket, held in place by a foot. (Author/1940s Swansea Bay)*

▼ *An as-new stirrup pump, shown coiled up for convenient hanging storage. The pump featured 30ft of hose length. (Author/1940s Swansea Bay)*

The Home Office's 'General guidance for dealing with fires' included the following points:

- Keep all doors and windows closed, as if room doors are left open a staircase could act as a flue for transmitting flames between rooms.
- If you have to open a door that might have fire on the other side (for example, if you want to spray inside with a stirrup pump), it was advised to place your foot a few inches from the door before turning the handle; on a door that opened towards you, this meant that the fire might suddenly thrust the door open but your foot would stop it flying into your face. The door would also shield you from the flames, heat and gases.
- When moving through a room, corridor or staircase that is burning or has been affected by fire, stay close to the walls, as these positions are stronger and less prone to collapse.
- In smoke-filled or heavily burning buildings, crawl along the floor where the air is clearer and less noxious, and visibility is better.

Extinguishing general fires usually involved playing the jet of water from the stirrup pump at the base of the flames, and soaking the surrounding areas to prevent spreading combustion. Tackling incendiary fires required more specialised techniques. Most important was to resist the temptation simply to throw a bucket of water over the sputtering device; this would cause an aggressive reaction, and result in the bomb exploding and throwing out fragments of burning magnesium with violent intensity. For much the same reason, *Air Raids* advised against using the stirrup pump jet to tackle the blaze.

Interestingly, there seems a little variation in advice on this topic. A Canadian booklet entitled *Incendiary Bombs and How to Deal with Them*, published in the early 1940s and drawing on the UK experience, states that a 'small jet' of water from the stirrup pump could be directed on to the burning bomb: 'Although the jet of water will cause the burning magnesium to scatter, experience has shown that this involves less risk of personal injury than might be expected. As a general rule, it is better and safer to use a spray.' Looking across other recommendatory documents of the era, the balance of advice seemed to be that if you were going to tackle the bomb with a stirrup pump, it was best to alternate between the jet and the spray, using the jet to dampen down fires started around the bomb while the spray was played on the bomb itself, to quench its fury progressively. The closest safe range to tackle the incendiary fire was 6ft. Official advice also recommended that three people be used to fight the fire: Number One would be in charge of the pump nozzle; Number Two was the stirrup-pump operator, who would aim to deliver 65 double-stroke pump actions every minute; Number Three would bring up fresh buckets of water, as large amounts of water (up to 6 gallons) would be needed to control such an intense fire.

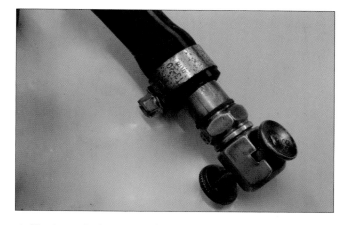

▲ The brass jet/spray nozzle of the stirrup pump. The jet setting allowed water to be projected up to 30ft, depending on the strength of the pumping. (Author/1940s Swansea Bay)

▼ Wartime visual instructions for fighting an incendiary fire with both a stirrup pump and a Redhill fire scoop. Note how the woman stays low to avoid the rising heat. (Author)

Although the use of the stirrup pump was explained in detail in British manuals, accompanied by rather decorous images of a family working together to tackle the blaze, the government advice tended to lean towards smothering an incendiary bomb as the best means of handling the threat. This would be performed by dumping loose earth, sand or ash atop the bomb, or covering it with a sandbag or sandmat. Because of the chemical nature of the incendiary, it was likely to keep burning even if entirely covered, but at least the fire would be mostly contained, unless it burned through a floor/ceiling. Of course, you had to get close enough to the scorching device to do this, and the government gave advice about the type of improvised and manufactured shields that could enable a stirrup pump operator (the one at the business end) or someone with a sandmat to move into fire-fighting range.

◀ *A TFLE hand-held fire extinguisher bottle. Both hand-pumped and gas-powered extinguishers were produced. (Author/1940s Swansea Bay)*

When a Bomb falls in the open....

Hold a Sandmat in front of your face....

Place it on the Bomb....

and get away quickly.

▲ *A cartoon illustrates, rather decorously, how to apply a sandmat to a burning incendiary. Note the central grip in image 3, to prevent burnt fingers. (Author/Joseph's Militaria)*

FIRE SHIELDS

The following is official Ministry of Home Security advice regarding the production of fire shields, taken from *Air Raids! What you must know, what you must do* (1941):

Tests have shown that almost complete protection against explosive firebombs and against flying molten metal can be obtained at all distances with a shield of 7/8in board not less than 28 ins. long and 20 ins. wide and backed with 22 gauge steel. The shield should have two peepholes 1 in. wide and 3/16 in. deep, one midway between the two sides and not less than 5 in. from the top, the other not more than 18 ins. from one side. At one side of the shield there should be a slot 3½ ins. long and 1½ ins. wide for the nozzle of the stirrup hand pump. The shield should have a handle fixed to the back and long enough for the shields to be held upright by anyone crouching while approaching a bomb or lying prone with one elbow resting on the ground.

This shield weighs about 15 lbs. and is therefore too heavy for the average householder. It is used chiefly by industrial fire parties operating in buildings of high fire risk. There are, however, various lighter shields which give useful protection, for example:

1. A solid or built-up 7/8 in. board backed by a dustbin lid or beaten-out corrugated iron or other thin plate gives a large measure of protection.
2. A ½ in. board similarly backed, or a 1/16 in. steel plate, gives for protection against flying pieces of burning magnesium and flying sand or soil, but is not completely proof against penetration by flying steel splinters at 15 feet (the maximum distance at which spray for a stirrup pump can be effectively used on a burning bomb).
3. A ¼ in. ply board, or a dustbin lid, or four thicknesses of folded wet blanket hung in front of the face over one arm gives for protection against molten magnesium and flying sand or soil but not against steel splinters even at a greater distance than 15 feet.

Many householders would also have bought or been issued with various incendiary 'scoops', essentially metal scoops, spades or cylindrical trapdoor devices used either to dispense sand on to the bomb from a safe distance or literally pick the bomb up and carry it outside the property. One of the most popular types was the Redhill ARP incendiary bomb scoop and hoe, which came in two parts that could be used separately or could be joined by a threaded connection to make a handle 7ft long. One section contained the large scoop, while the other was fitted with a hoe. The idea was that the fire-fighter would use the scoop to cover the bomb with sand, smothering it, then use the hoe section with the other hand to drag the bomb and any other burning debris into the shovel for removal. The Redhill container was another piece of useful equipment – a hinged metal sandbox into which the red-hot incendiary could be dropped.

Needless to say, the reality of tackling an incendiary bomb fire was rarely done so neatly in genuine attacks. Because of the number and distribution of incendiary bombs, homeowners might be overwhelmed by multiple devices puttering away in their own property. If these couldn't be controlled within about two minutes, and there were plenty of combustible materials for the fire to feed on, then the home might quickly be gutted, the occupants having to flee for their lives. Furthermore, many incendiaries would lodge themselves in high, inaccessible places, such as roof spaces, with limited access for the would-be fire-fighter. (After raids, schoolchildren became adept at spotting houses hit by incendiary bombs, because of the exposed and charred roof rafters; properties affected by HE, by contrast, would have bulging, collapsed or sheared walls.)

At the same time, the hapless family might also have to cope with the devastating impact of HE bombs. In the case of an uncontrollable fire, if it were impossible to exit via the doors, the citizen was encouraged to leave from windows. If the windows were upstairs, the advice was to hang from the windowsill by the hands before dropping to the ground, to reduce the drop.

▼ *The Nuttall Incendiary Bomb Scoop had a hinged cylindrical box on the end of a long operating arm, and was used to pick up incendiaries. (Author/1940s Swansea Bay)*

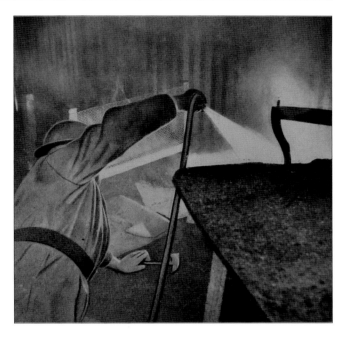

▲ *An instruction manual image shows a rescuer spraying an incendiary. It was recommended to work up to within 6ft of the bomb. (Author/Joseph's Militaria)*

▼ *Using an incendiary scoop, this householder is depositing a burning incendiary bomb in a Redhill Sand Container, a lidded metal box to smother the device. (Author)*

HIGH-EXPLOSIVE ATTACKS

BOMB TYPES

The majority (eight out of ten) of the HE bombs dropped on Britain during the Blitz were of the *Sprengbombe Cylindrisch* (SC) family, general-purpose types used for demolition effects on unprotected buildings. They came in a series of increasing sizes, designated according to the weight of the munition in kilograms: 50, 250, 500, 1,000 and 1,200kg *Hermann*, 1,800kg *Satan*, 2,000 and 2,500kg *Max*. There was also the semi-armour-piercing *Sprengbombe Dickwandig* (SD) types (50, 70, 250, 500 and 1,700kg) and the fully armour-piercing *Panzerbombe Cylindrisch* (PC) family (500, 1,000kg *Esau* and 1,400kg *Fritz*), the SDs and PCs used to attack 'hardened' targets such as industrial harbour facilities and protected military installations.

The volume of ordnance that could be carried by the individual German warplanes varied according to the type of aircraft. Thankfully for the British, the Luftwaffe never convincingly developed a long-range fleet of four-engine strategic bombers capable of carrying very heavy bombloads, such as the British Lancaster or the US B-17 Flying Fortress. Instead, they relied primarily on two-engine medium bombers, especially the Heinkel He 111, the Dornier Do 17 and the Junkers Ju 88. The Do 17 had a maximum internal bombload of only 1,000kg, the Ju 88's was 1,300kg and the He 111, the true workhorse of the Blitz, could transport 2,000kg. The mix of bombs carried depended very much upon the mission parameters and the intended targets. A typical Do 17 load during the earlier stage of the Blitz was 20 × SC50s or 4 × SC250s. As the Blitz went on, it

▼ *A German 250kg bomb. The holes on the body of the bomb indicate where fuses have been removed. (High Contrast/CC BY 2.0 DE)*

became increasingly common for German bombers to be equipped with fewer, heavier types, as we saw in the case of the bombing of my father's street in 1941, the He 111 disposing of two SC1000s.

Looking to amp up the destructive force of their HE attacks, from mid-September 1940 the Luftwaffe also began dropping the 500kg *Luftmine A* (LMA) and 1,000kg *Luftmine B* (LMB). Both of these were actually sea mines, usually dropped into the waters around the UK and detonated by magnetic or acoustic underwater detonators. These weapons, however, had a very high charge/weight ratio of 60–70 per cent explosive content – far higher than the conventional bombs. They were fitted with 27ft-diameter green artificial silk parachutes and impact fuzes. Known by the British as 'Land Mines', these weapons were utterly inaccurate; their parachute deployment ensured that they were blown over a wide area. However, their destructive effects more than made up for their inaccuracy. Because of their slow descent (c. 40mph) and their rounded body shape, they did not penetrate on impact, meaning that the ground did not absorb a significant proportion of their blast effect. A clockwork time fuse would trigger the instant the nose hit a solid surface, and c. 25 seconds later the explosive would unleash a huge detonation, creating overpressures that were capable of bringing down heavy concrete buildings.

The tactical effects of the German bombs could be adjusted through the type of fuse fitted. The most basic type was the 'instantaneous fuse', as the British authorities called it, which detonated a bomb the very instant it made an impact. More nefarious were the time-delay fuses, which as the name suggests exploded the bomb after a pre-set time delay following surface contact. This delay could be a matter of just a few seconds, long enough for the bomb to

▲ *This London double-decker bus was wiped out in a raid on the capital on 10 October 1940. Observe the vehicle's roof lying by the side. (AirSeaLand Photos)*

penetrate through a few floors of a building before detonation, increasing the likelihood of building collapse. Alternatively, the delay could be adjusted, depending on the type of fuse, from a few minutes to several hours and even to periods of days. The purpose of such longer fusing was twofold. First, when the explosion did finally occur, it was more likely to catch Civil Defence workers tackling fires and other emergencies in the vicinity. Second, the presence of a time-delay bomb or indeed any sort of UXB meant that entire streets or buildings would be out of commission until the devices were made safe. The citizens of blitzed cities found they had no access to undamaged homes, or were obliged to take long and time-consuming diversions to work, costing productive hours. Anything to disrupt the life of the cities.

▶ *Various officials gather around a Luftmine B parachute-dropped German mine. Such devices detonated either by impact fuse or magnetic disruption. (AirSeaLand Photos)*

UXB TEAMS AND BOMB DISPOSAL

It is estimated that about 10 per cent of the thousands of German bombs dropped on Britain failed to explode. The job of finding, unearthing, defusing and removing the unexploded bombs (UXBs) fell to the strong-willed men of the Bomb Disposal (BD) units. Their job was made more nerve-shredding by the fact that of a daily average of 84 UXBs dropped over Britain during the Blitz months, seven would actually have delayed-action fuses, and so would detonate at a time unknown, certainly unknown to the men who had to kneel by the bomb's side during defusing. Also, as the Germans became wiser to the efforts of BD crews, they introduced various anti-handling devices, designed to explode the bomb if it were moved or the BD team attempted to extract the fuse. It was a cat-and-mouse game without forgiveness, and one that frequently killed the BD crews, with many brave individuals utterly vaporised by their proximity to the blast. Yet in total, by war's end, the BD crews had defused 60,000 devices.

During the Blitz, the vanguard of UXB removal were 25 BD companies, part of the Army's Royal Engineers. Each company was formed into 10 sections, and each section had a BD officer in charge and 14 assisting ranks. Bomb disposal itself was a practice requiring extensive training and a methodical approach to risk. In outline, the first step was to identify the location of a UXB. The bomb might be lying in the open, or atop rubble, but often the only indication was a hole in the ground or in the side of a building. Typically, the size of the hole was about 2in or more larger than the bomb making it. Holes of 8–12in indicated a 50kg bomb; 14–18in a 250kg bomb; and over 18in a 500kg bomb or larger. Any holes under 6in in diameter were typically not made by bombs. The depth of bomb penetration into the ground could be anywhere up to 60ft, depending on the type of bomb and the material/ground through which it travelled, but the majority would be found within 25ft of the surface. Note that the tail fins of the bomb were often pulled off during penetration, so these were not a good indicator of the location of the bomb itself.

Once a bomb location had been identified, the next step was to work with ARP services to cordon off the area, evacuate civilians and prepare buildings in the vicinity for a possible further explosion (opening windows, opening outer doors, shoring up unstable structures, sandbagging nearby basement walls etc.). It was especially important not to allow any heavy wheeled or tracked vehicles into the vicinity, as the vibrations they emitted could set off a motion-activated fuse. Once preparations had been done, the BD team would then dig down to the bomb, with extreme caution, uncovering the bomb sufficiently to identify its type, and hopefully its fuse, and create enough space to work on the device. After an initial assessment,

▲ *A bomb disposal team, accompanied by onlookers, uses a crane to winch out a threatening-looking SC1000 bomb. (AirSeaLand Photos)*

the team had to make a decision about whether to attempt to defuse the bomb or, if that was too dangerous, simply detonate it in situ, after heavily packing it with sandbags to mute and deflect the blast.

Defuzing was thus a time-consuming and perilous occupation, a mental battle with the engineer who designed the bomb and fuse. Clockwork time fuses, for example, could be stopped by using powerful magnetic devices or by hydraulic 'clockstoppers', which pumped viscous oil into the fuse mechanism to arrest the clock's balance wheel. There were also special wire reels used for drawing out electric fuses from a distance, or simply old-fashioned spanners or locking wrenches to defuse bombs by hand, the BD expert's body often pressed hard up against the bomb case. The ideal outcome was for the fuze to be removed clear of the bomb, after which the bomb could be winched out of its hole, placed on the back of a truck, and taken away for safe disposal.

▶ *Unexploded German ordnance remained a threat well after the end of the war, indeed to this day. Here two men attempt to defuse a bomb from the bottom of St James's Park lake in February 1946. (AirSeaLand Photos)*

BOMB EFFECTS

The urban British soon became very familiar with the lethalities and sensations of HE bombs' detonations. Single bombs could have quite disproportionate and horrific consequences. During a raid on London on 14 October 1940, for example, a large bomb fell on the road above Balham Tube station in south London, at a time when some 600 people were sheltering in the tunnels below. The blast was so raging that it tore a crater 60ft wide in the road, and deep enough that a double-decker bus literally dropped into it, the crater depth as great as the length of the bus. The shock waves tore open the underground tunnel beneath, but also caused millions of gallons of sewage to flood the passages, along with hissing gales of gas from fractured mains. The combined toll from either blast, drowning or gassing, or a combination of all, was 68 people killed.

If a large number of people were in a relatively unprotected structure on ground level, the consequences could be even more dire. In September 1940, the South Hallsville School in Agate Street, Canning Town, had been established as a rest centre for traumatised refugees from bombed-out areas. The school's basement was used as a shelter, but with more than 600 people in the building, the upper corridors and classrooms were also packed. The school was far from structurally sound, its old brick walls frail against possible bomb strike, as many people were nervously aware. For three days and nights, the bedraggled men, women and children were kept in the school, even as prominent local citizens harangued government officials about the dangers. Buses were scheduled to arrive to transport the school's occupants out of the area, but they did not turn up, either because they simply omitted to or because they were sent to a wrong address in Camden Town, rather than Canning Town. Either way, at 0345hrs on Tuesday 10 September, a German bomb scored a direct hit on the school, the whole building collapsing in one devastating instant. Rescue services subsequently worked tirelessly under the most terrible conditions for 12 days, trying to find survivors but more frequently collecting bodies and gory fragments thereof. The total death toll was c. 450, from just one bomb. (Evidence suggests that the bomb might actually have been a parachute-deployed landmine.)

BLAST EFFECTS

Following examples of random powerlessness before death, it might seem churlish to talk of bombing survival techniques, but instructions were given about ways of maximising survivability. This advice was particularly important to the Civil

▼ *Despite the dark night, London is brightly illuminated by the hundreds of fires burning across the city, seen from miles away. (AirSeaLand Photos)*

Defence personnel, as they would remain largely above ground and on the streets during raids, often in close proximity to explosions. *Air Raids* described four specific types of effect from HE bombs:

Earth shock – A kind of 'localised earthquake', 'earth shock' was essentially the explosion's concussive shock waves travelling through the ground and nearby structures. The shock waves were not only capable of destabilising or even bringing down walls and buildings, but they also often fractured water mains, gas pipes and other underground utilities. In fact, a major cause of death of citizens trapped in collapsed buildings was either drowning or being gassed by such effects.

Blast – A bomb creates its effect through massive gas expansion, with an explosive velocity of between 2 and 6 miles/sec. The outer edge of the explosion, the initial shock wave, and the further supersonic shock waves that follow in its wake (these are essentially the air in rapid movement), inflict material and human damage instantly, especially as they are often accompanied by heat and lethal fragments. The outrush of air from the explosion also creates a vacuum, resulting in a secondary inrush of air back to the explosion site, this creating a powerful suction that drags with it wound-causing fragments.

▼ *The morning after. Streets were so transformed by the bombing that often people became lost in once-familiar home neighbourhoods. (AirSeaLand Photos)*

Injuries and morbidity vary with the proximity of the citizen to the epicentre of the blast and their access to shelter and protection; those several hundred yards away might experience little more than severe bruising, while those within a few yards could literally be vaporised. Some myths abounded among the Blitz community. The *Air Raids* manual was quick to point out that 'The impact of the blast wave on the body wall may cause bruising of the lungs and sometimes other organs, but serious or fatal injury directly attributable to blast is likely only very near indeed to the bomb. The view that blast causes internal injury by forcing its way into the body through the mouth or nose, or sucking air out through the mouth and nose, has been discredited.' This view was typically based on the not uncommon experience of finding people killed by bombing with not a mark on them, and appearing to all intents and purposes as if sleeping peacefully. In fact, such injuries tended to be the result of the blast causing internal traumatic brain injury or pulmonary contusion – bruising or bleeding of the lungs, leading to fluid build-up that eventually causes death by hypoxia (oxygen deprivation). The latter malady could cause death several hours after an explosion, despite an individual initially walking away from the explosion apparently unharmed.

In their material effects, bomb explosions often seemed to defy logic. Craters could seem preternaturally large, especially if they had caved in some subterranean structure. When a bomb fell on Bank tube station on 11 January 1941, for instance, the crater measured 200ft across; a bridge actually had to be built across the gap to keep traffic moving in the

THE EFFECTS OF A 1,000KG BOMB

Recent scientific and material tests of explosive effects provide some data on the potential human and material impact of an SC1000 aircraft bomb:

- At the impact point of the bomb, a crater c. 45ft in diameter is produced. Within this area, the destruction to both material and people is absolute, with a likely 100 per cent mortality.
- At a distance of 100ft from the blast, in all directions (depending of course on any physical features that might redirect and control the blast), the overpressure remains lethally high (approx. 30psi). Most buildings are destroyed (even those built of reinforced concrete)

and most people killed within this radius, although with adequate shelter some individuals will survive.
- As the distance from the centre of the blast increases, the bomb pressure begins to drop, but it still remains lethally high for considerable distance – the blast radius of an SC1000 bomb is around 1,200ft. Even a pressure of 5psi will cause destruction of conventionally built residential properties, and such properties may suffer significant damage at just 2psi.
- There will be lethal fragmentation within the blast radius, but death and injury from this source can be encountered much further, even as much as 1,250 yards away.

area (111 people were killed in the detonation and subsequent tube tunnel collapse). One house might be nearly wiped from the face of the earth, whereas another proximate building might almost inexplicably be apparently untouched. *Air Raids* acknowledges and explains the fact that bombs might deliver 'freakish results. This is due to the combined and contradictory effects of pressure and suction, and to the way the blast wave may be deflected from walls and other unyielding surfaces.' This is why some particularly important buildings during the Blitz had blast walls and 'baffles' erected around them, designed to deflect and interrupt the blast and thereby minimise damage.

Splinters – What the *Air Raids* manual referred to as 'splinters' was specifically the metal fragments of the bomb casing, fractured into thousands of jagged metal pieces on detonation and hurled outwards at supersonic speeds. British government studies found that shrapnel could penetrate 2in steel plate. Illustrating the power of such shrapnel, turning back to my father's single bombing incident, a single piece of shrapnel from one of the bombs had gone through the McNab family's garage wall, through the entire car inside, out the other garage wall and stuck in a fence. The piece was still warm when Brian touched it, hours later. Nor did the splinters always follow predictable flight paths; they might easily ricochet and be redirected off hard surfaces. Generally speaking, however, the fragments would fly upwards and outwards at an angle to the floor, the extent of that angle dictated by factors such as the depth to which the bomb penetrated before exploding.

In addition to generating splinters, a bomb blast would also turn surrounding materials into lethal projectiles, including stones, splintered wood and metal artefacts. One of the biggest dangers was laceration injuries caused by shattering

▶ *How to rescue an unconscious person from a burning room. The victim's wrists are tied behind the rescuer's neck. (Author/Joseph's Militaria)*

and falling glass; a single large bomb might put out every single window within hundreds of yards. Being struck by glass caused a variety of injuries, from life-threatening major open wounds to hundreds of little pinprick injuries dotted across the body.

Fire – The final major threat from HE bombs was fire, not so much from their own blast effects but more from the fracturing then ignition of gas mains. There was also the fact that the vast majority of homes in the UK during this period were lit by coal fires, and if a building was hit by a bomb then burning coals could be whipped out from the fire, or household debris might drop into the hearth. It was for this reason the government recommended that fires be kept damped down during an air raid, not always an easy instruction to comply with on freezing winter nights.

▲ *A rescue worker demonstrates how to shovel sand on to an incendiary using a long-handled scoop and a sandbox. (Author/Joseph's Militaria)*

▲ *An idealised view of a civilian couple in 'anti-gas' clothing, consisting of high-necked oilskin coats and hats and rubber wellington boots. (Author)*

SURVIVING THE BOMBS

As might be expected, government advice for surviving HE bombs was rather more limited than that for tackling incendiary weapons – it was impossible to 'fight' a bomb blast, just attempt to survive it. As already noted, the best survival measure was to be in a substantial shelter, but for a wealth of reasons many citizens would nevertheless find themselves in exposed positions during air raids.

If the citizen was inside their own home and a raid began, they were advised to take immediate precautionary measures:

- Dampen down any burning coal fires (as noted above).
- If possible, turn off the gas at a mains tap.
- Position themselves in the house against an interior wall and out of a direct line with windows and doorways.
- Open the windows wide; this made them less prone to shattering under bomb concussion, and if they did, the glass fragments would not be hurled inside the house under pressure.

It was recommended that hearing be protected from damage with improvised ear protectors, made from plugs of cotton wool, smeared with Vaseline for easy insertion, twisted into the ear to form a protective plug. When bombs were falling close, the person should keep their mouth open, to equalise the blast pressure; parents were told that it was a good idea to have a stock of hard-boiled sweets at hand, to give to their children during a raid – the sucking action

kept the children's mouths opening and closing, thus guarding their hearing.

If the citizen was outdoors, and caught in a raid, the most basic expedient for surviving the bombs was to lie on the ground, which minimised the amount of the body exposed to fragmentation, or even better, find oneself a ditch, trench or similar depression to lie in. To avoid the worst effects of earth shock, the person should be 'lying face downwards, resting on the elbows, hands clasped behind the head and chest slightly raised from the ground'. Similarly, if the person were sheltering under a structure such as a railway arch or behind a wall, it was dangerous to lean directly against a surface. If you had to stand close to such a surface, a rolled-up coat, cushion or similar padding should be placed between you and the hard surface.

To clarify matters for the public, the Ministry of Home Protection graded the various locations and physical positions according to their relative risk, starting with the most dangerous and ending with the least dangerous. The scale was as follows:

1. standing in a street
2. lying in a street
3. lying behind low cover or in a doorway
4. sheltering in a house or other place affording head and side cover away from windows
5. in an Anderson shelter, covered trench, strutted basement or surface shelter

Overhead cover was not just important for sheltering from bombs. Another significant threat to the citizens of a blitzed city was the constant rain of fragments from the shells of British anti-aircraft guns, which either exploded high above the city or which sometimes didn't explode, and fell to earth as virtual bombs in their own right. Civilians soon learned to tell the difference between bomb fragments and AA shell fragments, because the latter often displayed portions of the copper driving band that went around the shell to engage with the gun barrel's rifling.

The influential publication *ARP* by S. Evelyn Thomas also provided details of the best material cover to survive the nearby impact of a 250kg bomb:

> The explosion of a 500-lb. bomb (the most likely size) in a 40-ft. wide street will blast down the front of brick and stone houses for a distance of 70 feet on each side, whilst flying steel splinters may cause death and injury within a distance of 700 yards.

> Full protection from the maximum splinter and blast effects of such a bomb exploding 50 feet away is afforded by 1½ inches of steel; or 13½ inches of solid bricks in cement; or 15½ inches of cavity bricks; or 12 inches of reinforced concrete; or 15 inches of ordinary concrete; or 2 ft. 6 in. of sand or earth.

> At a greater distance from the point of explosion the protective material can be less thick. At 100 ft., for example, a 9-inch brick wall is sufficient.

Such precision advice, it has to be said, was as much an act of hopeful reassurance as it was scientific advice. As those in the Blitz zones soon discovered, the power of modern HE weapons was so violent that nowhere gave a categorical assurance of safety (the deepest underground stations were

▲ *This scene in Coventry, 14 November 1940, shows complete building destruction. More than 550 people were killed in this raid. (AirSeaLand Photos)*

probably the best of all places to be). During a raid on Merseyside on 20–21 December 1940, for example, a large number of people took shelter under the muscular haunches of a large railway viaduct; a direct bomb hit on the structure simply collapsed tons of brick on to those below, killing 42 people. There was a randomness and violence to the Blitz attacks that no amount of advice could strip away.

▼ *This diagram explains how to escape from a second-storey window, the man hanging full length to reduce the height of the drop. (Author/Joseph's Militaria)*

▼ *Bomb fragments could retain lethality for hundreds of yard from the blast. The ribbed piece at the bottom is likely from a British anti-aircraft shell. (Author/1940s Swansea Bay)*

CHAPTER FOUR

CIVIL DEFENCE ORGANISATIONS AND DUTIES

At first, those volunteering for ARP/Civil Defence duties were sometimes publicly regarded with a mixture of humour and scepticism, a wry smile towards those 'playing at soldiers'. Such light-hearted regard disappeared altogether during the Blitz years, when those serving in Civil Defence roles directly faced combat at levels experienced by few frontline soldiers at this time. The cost to them was real – almost 7,000 Civil Defence workers were killed during the war. But without the 1.5 million men and women who gave themselves to such duties, it is hard to envisage how Britain would have continued to function.

▶ *A Heinkel He 111, seen moving over the Thames in London. Britain was fortunate that Germany only focused on two-engine medium bombers, rather than four-engine heavy bombers. (Shutterstock)*

OVERVIEW

As a concept, Civil Defence first took shape in 1924, with the establishment of two Air Raid Precautions (ARP) subcommittees (the Ministerial Committee on Policy and the Official Committee on Organisation) as part of the Committee of Imperial Defence. The remit of the ARP bodies, headed by Sir John Anderson (the Lord Privy Seal), was to examine how the British nation could achieve 'the organisation for war, including Civil Defence, home defence, censorship and war emergency legislation'.

For the first nine years of their existence, much of the work of the ARP subcommittees was dutifully theoretical. With Hitler's ascent to power in 1933, however, a new seriousness focused minds, and in March of that year the subcommittee issued instructions to Britain's local authorities, highlighting their practical responsibilities for setting up Civil Defence structures. In 1935 – by which time German remilitarisation was in full swing – the government upped its commitment to ARP preparations by establishing the ARP Department, directly within the Home Office (the ARP subcommittees were dissolved in 1936).

▼*An emergency services training drill sees two rescue workers lower a simulated injured man from an upstairs window. (AirSeaLand Photos)*

ORGANISATION OF THE ARP DEPARTMENT (1939)

Deputy Under-Secretary's Branch (administrative)

Responsible for: ARP policy and legislation; parliamentary and establishment matters

- J Division (approval of statutory schemes)
- L Division (protection of public utilities; secretarial work for the Committee of Imperial Defence committees and the Heads of Divisions Council)

Inspector General's Branch (technical)

Responsible for: organisation, training and inspection of local authority Civil Defence units.

- Training and Technical Division
- Supply Division
- Chief Inspector's Division (responsible for the regional inspectorate)

Other significant branches/divisions

- Research and Experiments Branch
- Division (air raid shelters)
- Chief Medical Adviser
- Chief Technical Adviser (later Chief Engineer's Branch)
- Chief Intelligence Officer
- Chief Instructor and Establishment Division

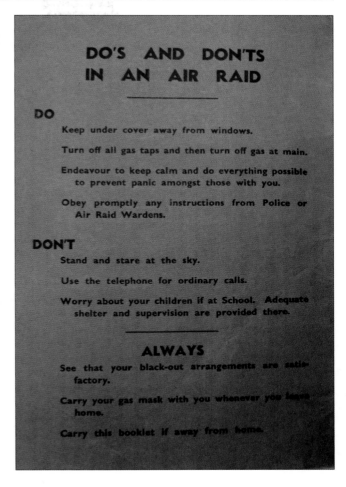

▲ *A booklet listing public shelters in Sheffield also explains the basic safety procedures during an air raid. Note the caution against standing and watching the raid develop – air raids were absorbing dramas. (Author/Joseph's Militaria)*

The crucial step forward in the development of Civil Defence was the ARP Act of 1937. In a nutshell, this lengthy and complex document transformed the local authority ARP preparations from the advisory to the compulsory. Each local authority had to prepare an ARP scheme – essentially a detailed plan of how the County councils would protect people and property from enemy air attack – and submit it to the Secretary of State for approval. Once the Secretary of State had given that approval, then the Act came into force locally.

The ARP Act undoubtedly imposed new financial and practical demands upon the local authorities, but they also acquired some special compensatory powers. For example, government grants (up to 75 per cent of the cost of the scheme) and special borrowing facilities were extended to help cover the new expenditure. Councils could make compulsory purchases of land, as would be required for air raid shelter construction programmes. They also began to recruit personnel.

The larger percentage of ARP workers were employed on a part-time basis, committing themselves to 48 hours of duties per month. This was a heavy additional commitment, especially once Britain began its transformation into a war economy from September 1939, with many workers putting in more than 50 hours per week at their regular job before

adding another 12 hours of ARP duties on top of that. At the height of the Blitz, those 12 hours of ARP commitments could seem like an optimistic dream; many citizens would find the hours available for sleep dizzyingly curtailed. For this reason, workers increasingly took on full-time ARP jobs at £3 per week (£2 for women).

In 1939, war was becoming a definite likelihood rather than an outside possibility, and this was reflected in further changes to ARP policy and structure. Based on the recommendations of the civil servant Sir Warren Fisher, a Minister of Home Defence was established, responsible for all matters pertaining to Civil Defence. Furthermore, Fisher proposed dividing the UK into 12 Civil Defence regions (see feature box overleaf), each under the authority of a regional commissioner, who was responsible for the coordination and later direction of Civil Defence schemes within the local authorities under his control. In September 1939, as war finally became a reality, a new Ministry of Home Security was established under the Ministers of the Crown (Emergency Appointments) Act 1939, a commanding

- Northern (HQ Newcastle upon Tyne)
- North Eastern (HQ Leeds)
- North Midland (HQ Nottingham)
- Eastern (HQ Cambridge)
- London
- Southern (HQ Reading)
- South Western (HQ Bristol)
- Wales (HQ Cardiff)
- Midland (HQ Birmingham)
- North Western (HQ Manchester)
- Scotland (HQ Edinburgh)
- South Eastern (HQ Tunbridge Wells)

▲ *S. Evelyn Thomas' ARP was one of the most consulted of the air raid publications, relevant for both citizens and Civil Defence workers. (Author/1940s Swansea Bay)*

◄ *A panel designating an air raid shelter. Similar signs featured directional arrows, pointing towards the shelter. (Author/ 1940s Swansea Bay)*

position that took the statutory powers of the Home Secretary, the Secretary of State for Scotland and the Lord Privy Seal. As well as a range of pertinent directorates, the Ministry had five specific departments:

- Air Raid Precautions Department
- Fire and Police Services Division
- Public Relations and Civil Defence Personnel Division
- Regional Organisation Division and the Home Security War Room
- Inspector General's Department

At this stage it is worth clarifying the breadth of organisations that took 'passive defence' responsibilities during the Blitz, as opposed to the 'active defence' embodied in Fighter Command, Anti-Aircraft Command and so on. The ARP Services (from late 1939 called Civil Defence General Services) included many frontline roles and responsibilities: report and control centres; engineer services (i.e. rescue, repair and demolition); anti-gas measures, including decontamination; ARP wardens and messengers; casualty services (first-aid posts/parties, stretcher parties, emergency ambulances, mortuary services); the Women's Volunteer Service (WVS); fire services (regional fire brigades, the Auxiliary Fire Service, Women's Auxiliary Fire Service, Fire Guards) and the police (regular, war reserve, special constables, Women's Auxiliary). Together, these organisations, and the people who served within them, could respond to the timeline of an air raid emergency from first detection of the approaching enemy aircraft to the post-raid clearance of debris. To make our analysis more manageable, in the remainder of this chapter we will focus specifically on police, ARP wardens and messengers, and key women's organisations. In the following chapter, the concentration will be more upon fire, rescue and medical services. Although this division is made, we must always bear in mind the truth that in the reality of war conditions, roles and responsibilities frequently blurred between organisations and between individuals.

THE POLICE

The police offered a useful pre-existing infrastructure for ARP services in the UK. With their deep knowledge of local communities, clear lines of authority and in-place procedures for dealing with emergency situations, they became integral to the air raid response, acting in every conceivable role from providing command and control through to rolling up their sleeves and working in rescue parties or alongside fire-fighting crews. They still had to maintain their responsibility for enforcing the law. The Blitz, contrary to music-hall patriotism, was not entirely a time of universal community spirit. As we shall see, crime found new and peculiar breeding conditions during the war. On top of that, the police were responsible for enforcing a whole new raft of wartime legislation, while also having to consider fresh domestic threats, such as enemy spies.

▼ *Two policemen guide a family around the site of an unexploded bomb. (AirSeaLand Photos)*

MANPOWER AND POLICE ORGANISATION

At the outset of the war, England and Wales had a total of 60,000 police officers, divided between 158 individual police forces, 58 county forces and 122 city and borough forces. The problem brought by war was that many men (only about 300 of the nation's police officers were women at this time) suddenly wanted to join the armed forces. Furthermore, significant numbers of the police were also military reservists, and therefore would be obliged to leave the police to join their particular unit of the armed services.

In September 1939, the government recognised the emerging problem and began to put in place measures to counter it. Restrictions were set upon the numbers of police who could resign for National Service, although it was seen that this measure was likely to be temporary, and only partly the solution to the problem.

▲ *The Group Warden, like other wardens, could offer his services to other sectors upon showing his official Card of Appointment. (Author/Joseph's Militaria)*

▼ *The instructions for correctly fitting and adjusting a gas mask became common knowledge for millions of UK citizens during the war years. (Author/Joseph's Militaria)*

yards apart, with a maximum of 10 posts per square mile. Less dense areas have fewer posts, but no built-up area should be more than a half-mile walk from a Post.' Each Post would be responsible for two, three or occasionally more (depending on the population density) Sectors, defined by certain streets or localities. The Posts were labelled by number and the Sectors by small letters. Thus a simple number/letter combination would give any warden a sense of where was being discussed. e.g. 'Sector A1 (a)' meant Sector (a) of Post 1, Group A. Five wardens would usually operate in each Sector, under the authority of a Senior Warden.

For towns and cities with populations exceeding 150,000, the structure was slightly different. These were split up into Divisions or Districts each with jurisdiction over about 80,000 people and headed by a Divisional Warden. Each Division would be divided into Groups, and thereafter the cascading structure noted above. The key point was that whatever the size of town or city, at street level all citizens would have an identifiable local warden Post and a committed group of local wardens, often citizens who were born and bred in the streets they monitored.

It is important to recognise that the wardens, as volunteer civilians, did not have a legal authority like the police. Yet Thomas thought it important enough to explain, with an emphatic use of bold font, that the wardens were 'an entirely separate corps under their own Chief Warden and do not form part of the police or special constabulary. **Whilst, therefore, wardens are expected to and must of necessity work in close co-operation with the Police, they are not subject to control by or to orders from ordinary members of the police force.**' Thomas may have felt it necessary to make this point to clarify, for ARP wardens, that they truly had to stand on their own two feet and make decisions for themselves; theirs was a position of independent action and confidence, not of subservient order-taking.

ROLES AND DUTIES

At the top of the tree for ARP wardens was the Chief Warden, who had overall responsibility for policy-making, recruitment, training, Post allocation and information distribution among the wardens. He would also have a body of reserve wardens under his direct control; these could be directed to support any beleaguered Post or Sector within the town. The Group Wardens were important figures in giving the personnel under their control a sense of shared purpose and collective morale. They would keep wardens fully informed of all developments and new instructions, often via monthly (or more frequent) meetings. These meetings would also be used to provide additional training and instruction. Group Wardens had further responsibility for matters relating to discipline and complaints.

One of the most important of the wardens was the Senior Warden, as the professionalism of his command would directly affect, at street level, the quality of ARP operations during an air raid. Thomas described the perfect Senior Warden: 'They should be alert, active capable men with some intelligence, who can be relied upon to act quickly and efficiently in emergency, and to control and regularly exercise the Wardens attached to their Posts.' Thomas then went on to list no fewer than 15 key duties of the Senior Warden, which included:

1. Supervision of his Post, including providing training, advice and instruction to the Sector Wardens.
2. Allocation of Sector duties and patrols.
3. Keep up-to-date records of the locations of ARP infrastructure within the Sector (fire hydrants, shelters, doctors, chemists, first-aid posts etc.) plus details of respirator distribution in the local area.
4. Produce a Sector map, and if possible distribute it to the wardens. A Sector map, given as an example for Senior Wardens, is reproduced on page 95.)
5. Maintain contact with all the Posts, including those in special locations, such as factories and offices.
6. Maintain contact with the Senior Wardens in all other Posts, to ensure the smooth local transfer of information.
7. To ensure that local citizens are provided with the best information about ARP measures and how to help themselves as much as possible in the case of a raid.

For the wardens themselves, the authority to perform their duties came following training and the issue of a 'Card of Appointment', a document signed by the Clerk of the County Council or the

▼ *ARP wardens, observed by a senior warden, demonstrate gas mask fitting to a group of bemused ladies in the first year of the war. (AirSeaLand Photos)*

Chief Constable that declared: 'This is to certify that [*name and address of warden*] has been duly appointed as an air raid warden.' With the granting of this document, the warden could then officially don the ARP uniform, badge and armlet.

Warden training was extensive. To perform his duties efficiently, he had to have a lot of information mentally, or physically (in written records) stored away, the product of both his training and his experience. According to official publications, the Air Raid Warden had to possess the following knowledge:

1. Understanding of poisonous gases, including how to detect them and protect against them.
2. The methods of tackling incendiary bombs.
3. How to protect against HE explosions, including the construction of private shelters and the provision of public shelters. (The warden was expected to direct people quickly and efficiently to the public shelters, so he needed to know their location and capacity.)
4. The techniques for fitting gas respirators. He would also provide guidance on local government distribution of respirators, helping to ensure that every citizen had one.
5. How to use and maintain the equipment supplied at the ARP Post.
6. A deep understanding of the local ARP and Civil Defence organisations and systems, including:
   - the sequence of local air raid warnings
   - address and telephone number of the Report Centre
   - contact details for police and fire services
7. An intimate awareness of the physical and practical layout

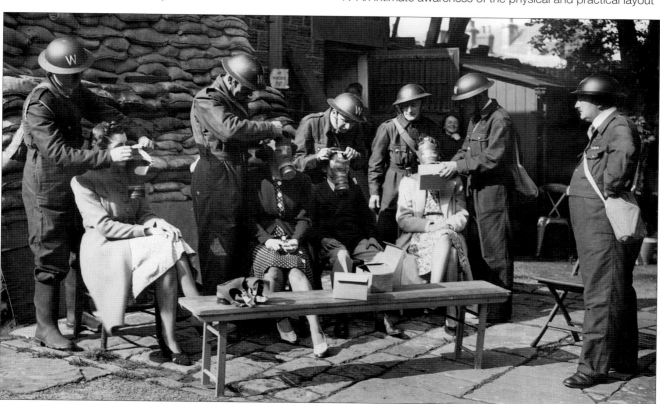

▲ *The Civil Defence patch was issued with the 'midnight blue' uniform, affixed on the chest of the official 1941 battledress blouse. (Author/Joseph's Militaria)*

▶ *A reconstruction of a warden's Post. Features here include a gas rattle, an 'all-clear bell' and reporting forms. (Author/1940s Swansea Bay)*

▼ *ARP warden Angelus on his rounds with his dog Rip, in an air raid shelter in Poplar, London, December 1941. (PD)*

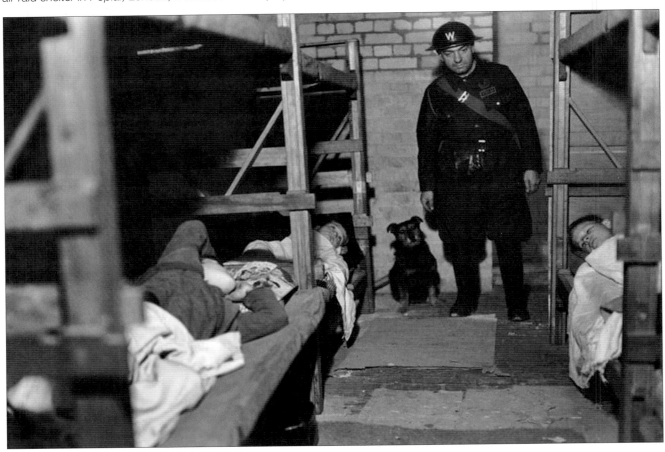

of his locale. Thomas' *ARP* manual lists some of the details as:

[. . .] the names of all streets and roads therein; the names, addresses and telephone numbers of his Group Warden, Senior Warden, and Sector Wardens, as well as of other stout-hearted people who might help in emergency; the addresses of invalids and infirm people who might require special assistance; the positions of the nearest Respirator Distributing Centres, Respirator Stores, Cleansing Stations, Decontamination Centres, First-Aid Posts, Ambulance Depots and Hospitals; the location of all water hydrants and other water supplies (ponds, wells, etc.); of police boxes and telephones; the addresses of all chemists, nurses, doctors and veterinary surgeons; the position of all public shelters, other places of safety, and places of special danger, such as petrol stores and timber yards; the situation of local means of cutting off escaping water and gas [. . .]

FACING THE RAID

When an air raid was expected, or when the warden was simply on duty, he had to report to his Post in his full duty uniform, carrying his personal issue equipment, which consisted of:

- protective overalls
- Civilian Duty Respirator
- steel helmet (usually featuring a capital 'W' on the crown), plus oilskin curtain
- eyeshield
- badge and armlet
- whistle
- electric torch
- gas rattle

The warden would stay at his Post until the 'Action Warning' alarm was given (see Chapter 3), at which point he would begin his patrols of the local area, often in the presence of another warden and possibly a messenger. (Note that one warden would be present in the Post at all times, to take responsibility for coordinating information with wider bodies.) As he walked about, the warden would use his whistle frequently as a warning, to supplement the sounding of the air raid siren. His main focus at this stage was to clear the streets, directing wandering civilians to shelters; this might also involve stopping vehicles and compelling the occupants to exit and get to safety.

Once this stage was complete, the raid was likely to have begun, and the warden switched his focus to reporting bomb damage or serious fires. Now began a period of events for which it was hard to be prescriptive about procedure, for the warden would largely be adapting to circumstances. They were told emphatically that they should avoid exposing themselves to unnecessary danger, and should obviously take cover when bombs were falling in the immediate vicinity.

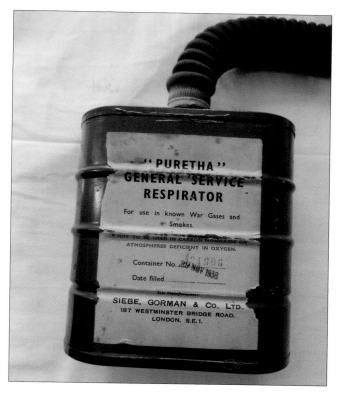

▲ The Service Respirator was provided to Civil Defence workers. The separate filter container gave the respirator longer protection and greater freedom of movement. (Author/Joseph's Militaria)

▼ A diagram of basic incendiary fighting kit. Wardens would also have a 10ft long 'ceiling pike', a device used to test weak ceilings or to bring them down. (Author/Joseph's Militaria)

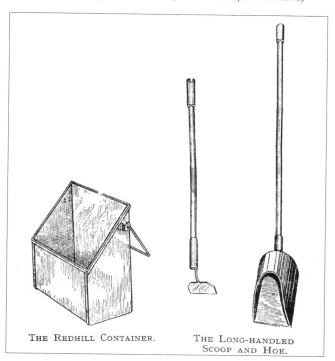

THE REDHILL CONTAINER.   THE LONG-HANDLED SCOOP AND HOE.

▲ *An ARP warden's metal storage box. The warden would use the box to store his personal kit plus some other minor Post equipment. (Author/Joseph's Militaria)*

Beyond that, the priorities were dictated by what was happening around them, the warden having to perform a mental triage regarding what was important. The advice given to wardens by Thomas was useful, and is therefore worth quoting at length:

ACTION ON AIR RAID DAMAGE

In emergency, you will have to use a great deal of common-sense in deciding what to do. **It is impossible to lay down rules that will apply to every case.** *So consider the position quickly, but carefully, and act promptly.*

Your actions should be ordered so as to SAVE LIFE FIRST,
1. **Succour any urgent casualties** *if you can, e.g. blister gas in eyes.*
2. **Prevent other casualties,** *e.g. by giving gas alarm, and keeping other people away from collapsing buildings.*
3. **Make a report** *to your Post.*

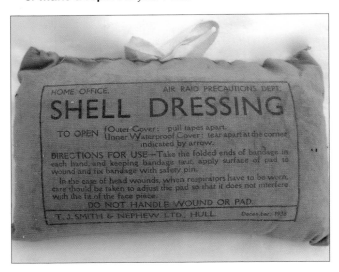

HOME OFFICE.   AIR RAID PRECAUTIONS DEPT.

SHELL DRESSING

TO OPEN {Outer Cover: pull tapes apart.
Inner Waterproof Cover: tear apart at the corner indicated by arrow.

DIRECTIONS FOR USE—Take the folded ends of bandage in each hand, and keeping bandage taut, apply surface of pad to wound and fix bandage with safety pin.
In the case of head wounds, when respirators have to be worn, care should be taken to adjust the pad so that it does not interfere with the fit of the face piece.
DO NOT HANDLE WOUND OR PAD.

T. J. SMITH & NEPHEW LTD. HULL.   December 1938.

If there is serious damage, danger or injury, at once call for help from other Wardens, police, special constables, etc., by several sharp blasts on your whistle, or by despatching a messenger to your Post, or by flashing your torch or handlamp.

You may have to decide whether to report to your Post for help or to render assistance to casualties. **Act on the basis that your duty is to save life and injury in your Sector AS A WHOLE.** *You must not delay getting an urgent report to headquarters, which may save many lives, in order to help one or two individuals.*

As is clear here, the injunction to save life involved the warden making potentially troubling and harsh ethical decisions. It also involved implementing measures that were partly taught to him during training and partly were the product of common sense. For example, if buildings were severely damaged and unstable, he needed to get any people in the vicinity away from the danger area. He would then block off the street approaches to the building, or any dangerous craters or unexploded bombs, by tying rope across the road. If he spotted an incendiary bomb burning high up in a building, he would tell the occupants (the presence of an incendiary was not always evident until it was too late) and evacuate them or work with them to extinguish the blaze, if that did not take him away from other important duties.

Whatever course of action the warden took, it was imperative that he filed a report of the incident as quickly as possible, sending the message to the warden manning the Post, who would in turn forward it to the Report Centre. The report could be filed either by a physical telegram, written in a duplicate carbon Report Book and hand delivered either by the warden or the messenger, or in the form of a telephone message. An accompanying photograph here shows a sample of the Report Book information, illustrating the type of information required. If the warden chose to file the message by telephone, the message had to be a model of concision and clarity. The following is a sample: 'Air raid damage. Warden's Post 15, Group C. Acme Factory, Highfield Road. HE and incendiary bombs. Seventeen casualties and others under wreckage. Serious fire. Water and gas mains damaged. Highfield Road partly blocked. 17:30 hours. Fire patrols 17–19 present. Front of works wrecked. Message ends.'

The thousands of Air Raid Wardens who patrolled Britain's cities saw a side of life that few could have predicted in the pre-war years. Those working in the worst-hit cities lived lives every bit as fraught as frontline soldiers, and like all ARP services, many paid with their lives, limbs and health.

◀ *A shell dressing. All ARP and Civil Defence workers would receive first aid training, and would likely use it for real in the Blitzed regions. (Author/1940s Swansea Bay)*

SPECIMEN WARDEN'S REPORT FORM

AIR RAID DAMAGE. Warden's Post No. 00   Group 00

Position of occurrence...

Type of bombs—H.E./Incendiary/Poison Gas/Smoke.....................

Approx. No. of Casualties (if any trapped under wreckage, say so)...............

....

If fire, say so...

Damage to mains—Water/Gas/Overhead Electric Cables/Sewers/Telephones......

Names of roads blocked..

Position of any unexploded bombs.......................................

Time :...

Services already on the spot or coming.................................

Remarks ....

ORIGINAL/DUPLICATE. To be used when report is sent by messenger.
  Delete whichever is inapplicable.

SECTOR INFORMATION CHART
To accompany Sector Map.

X.   **Cinema**—Danger point—panic—evenings and afternoons. Corner Cannon Street and Bedford Road.

P.S.   **Public Shelter**—Corner Cannon Street and Bedford Road. Attention needed here at warning.

S.   **School**—Corner Albert Road and Duke Street. Danger point during school hours—trenches for children provided 100 yards up George Street opposite.

T.   **Timber Yard**—Corner George Street and Albert Road—Fire Danger.

F.   **Factory**—Corner Hale Street and Albert Road—Chemical Works—grave danger of explosion.

Y.   **Garage**—Petrol Store—special fire danger. Corner Eton Street and Albert Road.

P.H.   **Public House**—possible danger point during opening hours.

D.1.   **Doctor** Forbes, 2, Cannon Street.

D.2.   **Doctor** Sims, 26, Duke Street.

C.   **Chemist**, Mr. Robinson, 16, Cannon Street.

I.   **First Aid Point**—Mrs. George, Member St. John, 29, Eton Street.

H.   **Fire Hydrants :** Albert Road, opposite No. 251, No. 269, corner Duke Street ; No. 278, Factory corner Hale Street. Bedford Road, opposite Public Shelter, corner Cannon Street ; No. 266, corner Duke Street ; No. 276, Cannon Street, opposite No. 6 ; No. 18, Duke Street, opposite No. 5 ; No. 20, Eton Street, opposite side entrance of Garage on corner ; No. 29, George Street, opposite side of Timber Yard on corner of Albert Road.

F.A.   **Fire Alarms**—Albert Road, opposite No. 235, corner Cannon Street ; No. 280. Bedford Road, opposite Dr. Sims, corner Duke Street.

P.B.   **Police Boxes**—Cannon Street, corner Bedford Road, outside cinema. Albert Road, corner Duke Street, outside School ; corner Hale Street.

WARDENS' PATROLS

1.	J. Jones.	ALBERT ROAD	S. side from 233 to Duke Street.
2.	R. Brown.	ALBERT ROAD	N. side from George Street to Hale Street.
			S. side from 269 to 291 inclusive.
3.	T. Smith.	CANNON STREET	Both sides.
4.	L. Black.	DUKE STREET	Both sides.
5.	M. White.	ETON STREET	W. side only from 1 to 33 inclusive.
6.	K. Davis.	BEDFORD ROAD	N. side only from 232 to Eton St.
7.	Mrs. F. Green will be stationed at the Post with **Mr. Harper**.			

▲ *The images on this page all show key reporting and reference ARP documentation. The form above was used to report bomb damage. (Author/1940s Swansea Bay)*

▶ *The Sector Information Chart corresponded with the Sector Map shown below. The chart listed important locations around the local area. (Author/1940s Swansea Bay)*

▼ *The Sector Map shows the Senior Warden's area of reponsibility. Note how the individual wardens are distributed for street-by-street coverage. (Author/1940s Swansea Bay)*

SECTOR MAP, POST 10. Senior Warden: James Harper, 11 Duke Street.

WARDEN'S POST

The ARP warden's Post could be located in almost any repurposed building, including rooms in domestic houses or office blocks. It was recommended that the Post have three specific spaces:

1. A reinforced and protected space, providing some degree of side and overhead cover from bomb blasts, debris or splinters. This room would also usually be prepared for sealing against gas attack. It was here that the Post would have its telephone, plus a table and lighting.
2. A space dedicated to storing the Post equipment, listed below.
3. A rest area, for wardens not on duty or recovering from their experiences. This space was not essential, however, and was frequently omitted.

The Equipment at a Warden's Post*
The following articles will be supplied *per warden*:–

- 1 armlet (of standard design)
- 1 steel helmet
- 1 Civilian Duty Respirator

In addition, public wardens' Posts will be supplied with the following equipment:–

On a scale as considered necessary:
- light oilskin anti-gas suits
- pairs rubber boots
- pairs anti-gas gloves
- anti-gas eye shields
- anti-gas curtains

A large manuscript book for recording occurrences.

- 3 electric torches
- 3 whistles
- 2 hand rattles
- 1 hand bell
- small first-aid box

[Elements not mentioned here but which were standard during the Blitz included:

- Report Forms
- stirrup pump and other fire-fighting equipment (such as Redhill ARP Incendiary Bomb Scoop & Bucket)
- spare respirators (for civilians who had mislaid theirs)
- telephone (or one nearby)]

*Given as listed in *The Duties of an Air Raid Warden* (1938)

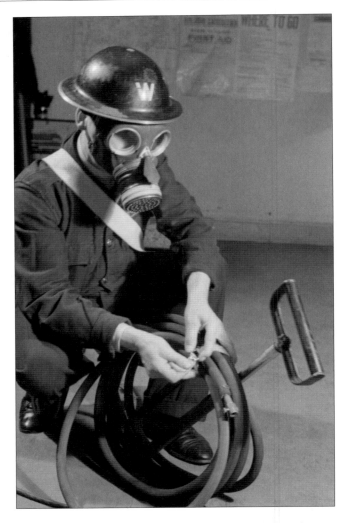

▲ *An ARP warden wears a gas mask as he crouches down to tie the hose of his Stirrup Pump into a neat loop at his Post. (PD)*

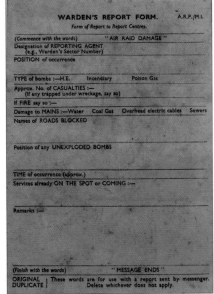

◄ *Another type of the Warden's Report Form. On receiving the information via messenger or telephoned report, the Report Centre would have to distribute and coordinate the information around the various emergency response agencies. (Author/1940s Swansea Bay)*

▼ *The rather nonchalant nature of this photograph of a warden's Post doubtless reflects the pre-war date on which it was taken (1 January 1939). During the actual Blitz, Posts were often directly under the bombing, and wardens themselves largely remained hazardously above ground for the raids. (Getty/Topical Press Agency)*

WOMEN'S SERVICES

The contribution made by women to Britain's war effort was incalculable. Here we shall focus on specific women's organisations that assisted in ARP duties, without taking in the broader but impressive involvement of women in areas such as the armed forces (unless they intersect with Blitz issues), agriculture and industry. We have already seen women involved in activities such as manning anti-aircraft positions and policing, but their involvement at the sharp end of the Blitz went far wider than those duties.

WOMEN'S VOLUNTARY SERVICE (WVS)

Even prior to war, the UK government recognised that women would have to be mobilised to a profound extent should conflict come to British shores, not least to assist in confronting the threat and consequences of a bombing campaign. In 1938, therefore, the Home Secretary, Samuel Hoare, approached Stella Hoare, the Dowager Marchioness of Reading (widow of the former Viceroy of India) and asked her to form a new women's Civil Defence organisation. Lady

▼ *Emergency Food Vans were a nutritional lifeline to both bombed-out civilians and to exhausted Civil Defence workers. (AirSeaLand Photos)*

Reading, by all accounts a formidable person with a long track record of running such bodies, set to the task with vigour, and the Women's Voluntary Service (WVS) was born.

Within six months, the WVS had 32,000 members, but during the war years membership rocketed to 960,000 – roughly one in 10 women in Britain. They could sign up for full- or part-time service, according to their availability. The list of the duties they performed was characteristically extensive for the times. They included:

- assisting with the evacuation of children, including billeting and welfare
- working as ambulance drivers and medics
- running Incident Inquiry Points (IIPs), which tried to reunite people separated during an air raid
- providing mobile canteens to both citizens and ARP personnel
- acting as marshals in air raid shelters
- establishing and manning rest centres for people bombed out of their homes
- assisting local authorities with effective food rationing measures
- creating mobile reading libraries

▲ *Ladies' gas mask containers, purposely designed into something a little more fashionable than the standard boxes or bags. (Author/Joseph's Militaria)*

▲ *A WVS rank badge and a sleeve insignia. The WVS uniform included a green skirt, coat and hat and a red blouse. (Author/Joseph's Militaria)*

- knitting woollen goods for soldiers and ARP personnel
- managing clothing collection and distribution, for people left without clothing following air raids
- providing administrative support in key local and national government offices
- supporting National Savings initiatives
- working in the Fire Guard

Although some of this list of duties might sound fairly benign, in fact the WVS women often found themselves directly in harm's way, delivering support to civilians and ARP workers under the flaming shadow of a burning building, or with bombs still falling nearby. The dangers of the role are indicated by the fact that 241 WVS members were killed during the war.

Structurally, the WVS had an organisation similar to that of the wardens, with a sequence of leadership descending from headquarters in defence regions (administratively the WVS followed this regional structure) down to the workers on the streets, essentially the WVS version of wardens. A sub-section of the WVS was the WVS Housewives' Service, which in 1942 became the National Housewives' Section. This organisation consisted of women who, typically, had family commitments that prevented them from signing up to the regular WVS. On an occasional basis, therefore, they still performed valued services, such as giving tea and company to bombed-out people or helping with gas-mask fittings, often from within their own homes.

AUXILIARY TERRITORIAL SERVICE (ATS)

The Auxiliary Territorial Service (ATS) was effectively the women's branch of the British Territorial Army, and was

▼ *An evocative photograph of a group of women at an Auxiliary Territorial Service (ATS) training camp. The ATS played vital roles in both Civil Defence and Air Defence. (AirSeaLand Photos)*

CHAPTER FIVE

FIRE, RESCUE AND MEDICAL ASSISTANCE

Almost every night during the Blitz, when the bombs began to fall, an army of emergency response workers raced into action. Fire-fighters, rescue services and medical teams had the shared and simple goal of saving lives, regardless of the danger that goal imposed upon their own lives and well-being.

◄ *Fire-fighters drive their truck through a wrecked street while water is played on the smouldering buildings to prevent reignition of fires many hours after the raid. (Shutterstock)*

FIRE-FIGHTING

THE AUXILIARY FIRE SERVICE (AFS)

As the UK became more war-minded during the 1930s, the British government considered the potential future requirements for fire-fighting services. At this time in history, and until the formation of the National Fire Service (NFS) in August 1941, Britain's fire-fighting capability was provided by county and regional services, each with its own training programmes, equipment and uniforms. These were adequate to handle local peacetime demands, but not the future threat of large-scale bombing. In 1937–38, therefore, the government passed a series of acts giving local authorities the power both to expand their existing brigades and to recruit men and women to a new volunteer fire service, to be known as the Auxiliary Fire Service (AFS).

The subsequent recruitment drive, heavily promoted via the press, posters and cinema, brought limited numbers of people initially, but during 1939 and 1940 the influx gathered pace impressively, so that the AFS rose to a strength of nearly

200,000 personnel. The inclusion of women as the Women's Auxiliary Fire Service (WASF) was a crucial component of this figure. Theoretically, women performed a number of support roles in the AFS, including driving emergency vehicles, manning emergency call centres and catering, but the situations confronting them at the scene of the bombing often meant that women became active fire-fighters, too. Regardless, WASF women had responsibility for countering fires that occurred in their own stations while the men were away, so they needed to be fully conversant with the fire-fighting techniques. All AFS members, men and women, underwent one month of training before they would be sent out on to the streets.

The AFS personnel were recognisable by their AFS lapel badge, which once the bombing started, they wore with

▼ *National Fire Service (NFS) fire and support engines of the type used in the Blitz; an Austin K4 with turntable ladder (left) and an Austin K2 towing vehicle. (Getty/Bert Hardy)*

pride (during the 'Phoney War', the AFS were regarded by some as dodging military service). They were issued with a blue double-breasted wool fire tunic and overalls and a dark-blue-and-red piped cap, also bearing the AFS lettering. They were officially part-time fire crew, although the racing demands of wartime meant that the difference between part-time and full-time fire brigade crews could be somewhat academic. This division produced some practical tensions. Regional fire brigades were issued with two uniforms, for example, whereas the AFS only received one; many AFS fire crews therefore went into their second or third night of calls in uniforms that were stinking, dirty and often still soaked from the spray of fire hoses.

NATIONAL FIRE SERVICE (NFS)

The National Fire Service (NFS) was formed in August 1941, after the main Blitz had subsided but when Britain still faced significant threats from German air attacks. One of the motivators behind the move was the experience of the Luftwaffe's switch of emphasis to more incendiary raids, which created storms of fire that often required the fire-fighting assistance of crews from outside the locale. While any help was welcome, this situation illustrated the problems of having numerous (c. 1,400) individual fire brigades, with different approaches to procedure and differing equipment types. For example, in London the brass fire hose 'branches' – the pieces that connect the hose to the hydrant – were of a screw-type fitting, whereas those of most fire brigades outside the capital had 'instantaneous' push-on couplings. It was clear that the UK's fire services needed some measure of standardisation if it were to become more effective.

The NFS was formed by making the AFS crews full-time fire personnel, while at the same time establishing more standardisation of practice and centralisation of control, with the NFS falling under the overall authority of the Home Office. Geographically, the NFS was divided into 12 Fire Force regions, these corresponding with the regional Civil Defence structure. Within these regions, the crews came under the authority of more than 40 'Fire Forces', each with a four-division strength and led by a Fire Force commander. With the effective nationalisation of the fire service, a national Fire Service College was born in Saltdean in Brighton, which served to standardise training and doctrine. The NFS was an instantly huge organisation. It rose to more than 350,000 personnel, and saw Britain through the rest of the war and into the post-war world.

SUPPLEMENTARY FIRE PARTIES, FIRE WATCHERS AND FIRE GUARDS

As effective as the combined AFS and fire brigades were, the government took further steps to ensure that the nation's fire service capabilities were maximised. The 1937 Memorandum

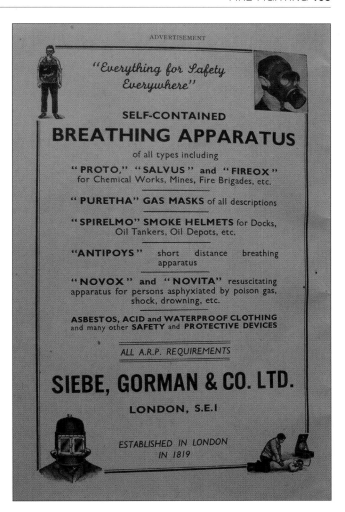

▲ *The list of breathing apparatus types in this advert indicate the range of threats to which fire-fighters were exposed during their duties. (Author/Joseph's Militaria)*

▶ *An NFS uniform, including fire axe and steel helmet. During an actual fire, the trousers (left) would usually be replaced by black oilcloth leggings. (Author/Joseph's Militaria)*

▲ *Taken just prior to the war, this photograph shows London fire officers using early forms of chest-mounted breathing apparatus. (Retired LFB/CC BY-SA 4.0)*

on Emergency Fire Brigades Organisation recommended the establishment of 'watching or fire posts', essentially small groups (three to five persons) of local volunteers trained (by the professional fire services) in core fire-fighting techniques and formed into Supplementary Fire Parties (SFPs).

The purpose of the SFPs was to offer a resource for fighting relatively small local fires, as might occur from an incendiary bomb. They were organised by local fire brigades and were generally equipped with a stirrup pump (750,000 pumps were manufactured for the SFPs) and basic buckets and hand tools, although some would later come to man light powered pumps. From the autumn of 1940s the SFPs also provided 'Fire Watchers', individuals posted to vulnerable or large-scale premises – whether commercial or governmental – to monitor and report fire outbreaks during raids.

The work of the Fire Watchers proved important and useful, but the reliance on part-time volunteers meant that there were problems with consistent cover. Therefore, the Fire Precautions (Business Premises) Order of 18 January 1941 obliged local authorities to make proper arrangements for fire watching and fire-fighting on important premises. Thus it was that all males aged between 16 and 60 working in such locations had to register for compulsory service, amounting to 48 hours per month.

The new arrangement was an improvement, but with the advent of the NFS in August 1941, it was seen that further organisational refinements could be implemented. The SFPs were therefore replaced with a national Fire Guard Organisation, the individuals therein known as Fire Guards. Much tinkering with practicalities followed, and following the February 1943 'Fire Guard Plan' every NFS fire station area would be divided into Fire Guard Sectors, and each Fire Guard Sector into Street Party Areas, the two subdivisions commanded by a Fire Guard Sector Captain or a Party Leader respectively. The Street Party teams were 20–30 persons strong, and essentially had a fire alert and fire-fighting responsibility over the streets in their immediate vicinity.

FIRE-FIGHTING EQUIPMENT AND VEHICLES

Personal equipment for the fire crews, apart from their uniforms, consisted of just the basic tools of the trade. A wide

▲ *This cigarette card image depicts a light trailer fire pump and fire fighter. The pump appears to be a Dennis trailer type of 1920s vintage. (Author)*

▼ *A recruitment poster for the Auxiliary Fire Service (AFS), which was targeted principally at those too young or old for military service. (PD)*

▼ *Pyrene Co. Ltd was a London-based fire appliance company founded in 1914. It also made hand-held extinguishers. (Author/Joseph's Militaria)*

FIRE-FIGHTING EQUIPMENT – GROUP FIRE PARTIES

The following equipment was listed for teams of six to eight fire-fighters in the government's *Incendiary and Fire Precautions* manual, 1939:

- 1 Light trailer pump
- 4 100ft lengths of 2¾in hose
- 2 75ft lengths of 1¾in hose
- 2 8 or 10ft lengths of suction hose
- 1 Dividing breeching
- 2 Branches with ⁵⁄₈in nozzle
- 2 Spare nozzles, one ¾in and one ½in
- 1 Canvas dam
- 20 Canvas buckets
- 1 Preventer
- 1 Felling Axe
- 1 Copper Suction Strainer
- 1 Basket Suction Strainer
- 1 Two-way suction collecting head
- Lines and small gear

and strong webbing or leather belt was worn around the waist, to which were attached a hemp line and a pouch for a fire axe. In London there would also be a pouch to carry a hose spanner.

The design of the fire axe was of note. In fact, there were two types. The first was a standard axe/pick combination with a handle made of ash wood. Yet a present danger to fire crews was electrocution – burning and collapsed buildings were often webbed with split or exposed electrical cables – so a special non-conductive fire axe was developed. This was known as the ARPAX, and was manufactured by Chillington Tool Company Limited of Wolverhampton. The handle of the axe was coated in thick rubber, which provided protection against shocks of up to 20,000 volts. A hand lamp was also a useful piece of kit, as

▼ *This Dennis fire trailer pump is being towed by a civilian vehicle, a common improvisation during periods of intense air raids. (Author)*

it was common for mains lighting to fail at the scene of a fire; mains electrical or fuel-powered 'hurricane' lamps were available.

Another important item of personal kit was the helmet. While many in the regular fire services had the pre-war cork-and-leather-type helmets, materials that also protected the wearer against electric shocks, the AFS had the rimmed military steel helmet. Although these gave no protection against electricity or heat, they were a) strong, b) easier to clean and decontaminate, and c) available. To provide additional protection to the helmet, an oilskin hood was attached, which covered the shoulders. This hood was originally intended to guard against gas, but it proved useful for repelling water, heat and sparks as well. The fire-fighter would don oilskins, overtrousers and jacket for the same reasons.

For fighting contained, unproblematic fires, small fire teams might utilise the standard stirrup pump, and they would also have multiple 2½–3-gallon canvas buckets for throwing water or sand on to contained blazes. Other useful bits of kit included a canvas dam sheet, for holding up to 20 gallons of water, and an 80ft lowering line, used for pulling hoses up to the top of ladders.

Delivering water on to flames required a pump to deliver the pressure. The most common types of pump were two-wheeled light trailer pumps. These were light enough to be towed into action behind a civilian car or truck, and not just a fire engine. Indeed, the AFS relied heavily on all manner of civilian vehicles to handle their emergencies; some 2,000 taxi cabs, for example, were hired for fire service at the very beginning of the war, their drivers often staying in the seat as AFS personnel.

The trailer pumps could deliver about 120 gallons per minute at 80lb pressure, and they came in a variety of models, some of which are pictured here as they appeared in contemporary adverts, posted in lucrative positions inside official government manuals. Typical examples include the Coventry Climax F.S.M. type Series 2 fire trailer. This had a single-stage centrifugal 241gpm fire pump, powered by a four-stroke, four-cylinder water-cooled 748cc petrol engine.

As well as numerous requisitioned civilian vehicles, the regular fire services could also use their professional fire trucks. There were several makes available, often conversions of standard commercial truck chassis. A classic example is the Austin K2 fire truck, which had a standard Austin truck chassis and was powered by a six-cylinder 28hp engine. The covered back of the truck had two benches, one either side, for seating a six- to eight-man team of fire-fighters. The bench seats were hinged, and the space beneath was used to store equipment, such as hoses and nozzles. To give the crew additional cover, the metal reinforced roof formed an overhead shield from shrapnel and falling debris. Some professional fire trucks had a fire pump built directly on to the flatbed, but the Austin towed a light trailer pump along behind it.

▲ An advert for a Coventry Climax ARP trailer pump. The pump could deliver a total water volume of 500 gallons per minute on to the fire. (Author/Joseph's Militaria)

▲ The Sportapool water reserves provided a mobile water solution for fire crews, offering 500 and 1,000 gallons of truck-mounted storage. (Author/Joseph's Militaria)

▲ Sigmund Pumps was also a manufacturer of stirrup pumps, as well as powered trailer pumps such as the one seen in this advert. (Author/Joseph's Militaria)

FIRE-FIGHTING EXPERIENCE

Fire-fighting during the Blitz was an experience shared only with those who have tackled the after-effects of bombing in other war zones. When major industrial centres were hit, fire-fighters had to face numerous, huge, multi-type fires within a single night, the fires often coalescing into unified blazes that covered acres. This situation was encountered especially around docks and ports, with the dockside warehouses, stored goods, shipping materials, oil and fuel depots, and local industries providing plentiful sources of fuel for the German HE bombs and incendiaries.

The scale of the ambient heat build-up could be terrifying. Telegraph poles burst spontaneously into flame, as did wooden block paving. Fire-fighters in London tackling a grain store blaze were faced with a scalding, swampy mass of melted grain sticking to their boots. On top of the heat came

LIST OF 'TRADES AND OCCUPANCIES WITH HIGH FIRE RISK'

- aeroplane store and manufacture
- artificial leather
- bedding manufacturers
- cabinet making
- candle making
- cardboard box making
- celluloid
- cellulose spraying
- chemical works
- cork – cotton wool
- cotton clothing
- cotton waste
- chemicals
- druggists (wholesale and manufacturing)
- dry cleaning
- film storage and handling
- fireworks
- flour and grist mills
- garages
- hay and straw dealers
- hemp, flax and jute
- India rubber manufacturing and treating
- insulating material
- manufacturing
- mould loft
- munition makers and storers
- oil and colour merchants
- oil and petrol stores (unless with underground tanks)
- oil refineries
- pattern shop and stores
- rag and waste dealer
- rag sorting
- repositories (furniture)
- rigger's loft
- sawmills
- ship's chandlers
- stationers (manufacturing)
- stables
- straw goods
- timber yards
- wood working

the concussions of bombs plus the periodic building collapse that sometimes killed entire fire crews.

One of the core problems of tackling Blitz fires was simply getting enough water on to the areas aflame. A large raid might demand the use of 500–1,000 individual water pumps; the typical number used for a major peacetime fire might be 20. When the mains water supply failed, the hoses were run into whatever water source could be found locally – rivers, ponds, water-filled ditches, etc. The reality was that on occasions, however, no amount of water was going to quench the flames, and if a conflagration could be contained – fire-fighters constantly played their hoses on nearby structures to prevent them igniting in a chain reaction – then the fire might just be left to burn out.

▲ *An incendiary ignites in a living room. The sputtering magnesium and thermite would quickly produce secondary fires on soft furnishings. (Author/Joseph's Militaria)*

▼ *An entire city block goes up in flames in Sheffield. Fire crews would be particularly vulnerable to eye damage in the super-heated, spark-filled air. (Author/Joseph's Militaria)*

RESCUE

The nightmare scenario for most people who endured the Blitz was not to be wiped out instantly in the sudden violent intensity of a bomb explosion, but rather to be buried under tons of rubble in a collapsed building, surviving in whatever precarious space prevented them from being killed instantly. People could and did make some remarkable survival efforts in obliterated structures, sometimes being freed several days after their sudden entombment. In most cases, however, the clock was ticking far more rapidly for those buried. If they had survived the initial building collapse, death might come within minutes or hours from injuries, suffocation (from being unable to breathe properly under the weight of debris), drowning (from the flooding caused by burst water mains), gassing (split gas mains) or fire. Their best chances of survival therefore rested in the hands of the Rescue Service.

ROLES AND ORGANISATION

As conceived at their establishment in the mid 1930s, Britain's Rescue Service had the following roles:

- locate, protect and extract people trapped within bomb-damaged buildings
- recover the dead from the same
- perform the necessary engineering/construction work to shore up damaged structures that are in danger of collapse, and in so doing might threaten further loss of life or obstruct important routes of traffic
- safely demolish unstable and damaged structures when necessary
- provide first aid when required
- assist the local fire services or other Civil Defence organisations when necessary

This dry list of duties only hints at the reality of Rescue Service work. In essence, the Rescue Services had to work endless frightening hours attempting to find and rescue people from beneath tons of splintered beams, concrete slabs, brick rubble and household objects, often in the dark and in the immediate vicinity of bomb explosions, fire, gas and water hazards and unexploded bombs. Like desperate cavers, they might frequently be called to crawl into rubble holes themselves to rescue people, the tottering remains of the building above threatening to come down at any moment. The dangers were endless, the experience psychologically wearing – the faint tap or feeble voice that indicated a living, trapped person might finally cease after hours of committed rescue effort, the end result being only a crushed body, grey from dust. It is little wonder that when King George VI instituted the George Cross (GC) on 24 September 1940 – essentially the civilian equivalent of the Victoria Cross – a high percentage of these went to the personnel of the Rescue Service.

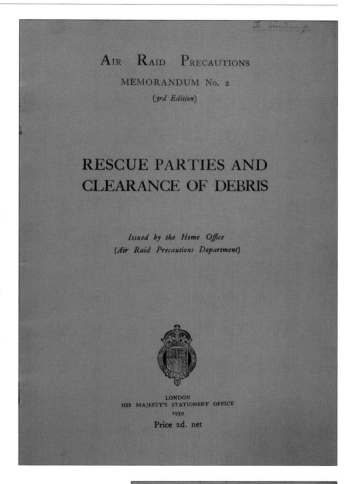

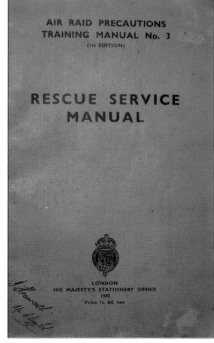

▲ *ARP No. 2 booklet provided detailed instructions on 'the extrication of casualties from buildings, etc., damaged by high explosive bombs'. (Author/Joseph's Militaria)*

▶ *The* Rescue Service Manual *(1942) was an extensive work describing all aspects of rescue operations. (Author/Joseph's Militaria)*

THE RESCUE PARTIES

Every local authority area would have a Rescue Service element, divided into teams known as Rescue Parties, stationed at Rescue Depots that acted as their command-and-control centres, as well as the locations where they stored all their equipment and vehicles. (The Rescue Depots might also be centres where other Civil Defence groups were based, the shared facilities enabling more fluid and rapid inter-agency control.)

Rescue Parties were divided into two types:

- Class 'A' – 'Heavy' parties intended for use at major incidents in vulnerable urban areas. Type A parties would be capable of handling substantial rescue engineering challenges, particularly major excavation work, and thus their equipment included industrial-scale jacks, oxyacetylene cutters, blocks and tackle and even cranes, if available.
- Class 'B' – The Class B 'light' Rescue Parties would attend smaller incidents requiring less in the way of engineering work, their equipment mainly consisting of hand-held tools, although one or more light parties might act in support of a heavy party when required. By 1941, the light Rescue Parties were more commonly found in rural areas.

Overall responsibility for the Rescue Parties in a district was a local authority matter. Each Civil Defence organisation would have a position such as 'Head of the Local Rescue Services', this individual usually being a senior local authority surveyor or engineer; his duties would include overseeing the recruitment and training of rescue personnel, the provision of proper equipment and the oversight of operational procedures. Administrative command at a Rescue Depot would normally rest in the hands of a Depot Superintendent, but both the

▼ *A casualty is carefully brought down from a rubble pile. Note the typical mix of ARP officials and civilians, although the latter might have building expertise. (AirSeaLand Photos)*

Head and the Superintendent would be expected to attend serious incidents when necessary.

The men who laboured in the Rescue Services were typically selected for their experience in the construction industry and engineering, as a good understanding of matters such as weight-bearing structures, material properties and utilities layouts could make the difference between life and death for both the rescuers and the people trapped. Many of the people came from within the local authority's own building and engineering departments, but civilian contractors were also recruited. Nevertheless, there were important differences between building work and rescue work. Training was essential. At first, training was a matter internal to the Depot. The *Rescue Service Manual* noted: 'Carefully planned, regular training must form part of the daily routine at every Rescue Depot. Although the Rescue Officers of the Local Authorities are responsible for the adequate training of rescue personnel under their control, Party Leaders [see below] are mainly responsible for the trained efficiency of their own teams, while Rescue workers themselves should make use of every opportunity for adding to and improving their practical knowledge of rescue technique. They can best do this by regularly witnessing, or, if possible, taking part in, actual rescue operations or demolition and clearance work.' As the last sentence here makes clear, much of the understanding of rescue work was acquired on the job, a reality necessitated as much by the pace of the bombing raids as by the lack of experience. Prior to the war, most of the limited understanding of rescue work was confined to those who had witnessed or written about earthquake rescue. As war realities became more pressing, regional training centres were established, and much later in the war, in 1944, a national Civil Defence Rescue School was established in Sutton Coldfield.

During the Blitz, each Rescue Depot would have at least two Rescue Parties stationed there, rotating in shifts so that at least one Rescue Party was always on standby; each depot would have facilities for sleeping, eating and washing. The recommended composition of a Rescue Party was 10 men, although in late 1941 (after the Blitz) five-person stretcher parties in London were converted to become light Rescue Parties; in 1943, the standard Rescue Party size changed again to seven people, apart from in London, which kept a five-person light and 10-person heavy structure.

Each Rescue Party was led by a Party Leader, a senior engineer or builder who also demonstrated the right leadership qualities – he not only would have to take control at an incident, but also had responsibility for his team's well-being and for matters such as discipline and reporting up and down the hierarchy of command. At an incident in which several teams were in attendance, the Party Leader of the team first on scene would have overall authority over the other teams. However, in areas of severe bombing Rescue Party Supervisors were appointed, specifically to take charge of multiple teams facing complex challenges. If the local Rescue Services Head were in attendance, his authority would 'supersede all others'.

Another important individual within the team was the driver. Heavy teams were assigned a truck for transporting its

▲ *A manual illustrates the correct way to bring a casualty down stairs without assistance, protecting the head as much as possible. (Author/Joseph's Militaria)*

▶ *A police officer demonstrates donning and carrying a gas mask in slung position (left) and alert position (right). (Author/1940s Swansea Bay)*

equipment, while light teams might have a small van or car, or even a hand-wheeled cart. Regardless of the vehicle, it was the driver's responsibility both to drive and to maintain the vehicle, and also to perform a range of other duties, including taking charge of loading/unloading of equipment from the vehicle, monitoring the return of equipment (largely to guard against theft) and completing the requisite log books relating to the journeys made (important for keeping track of fuel consumption).

The other men of the team would ideally be a group of building experts with mixed skills – plumber, carpenter, bricklayer, electrician, etc. They were a mixture of full-time and part-time workers. The part-time workers would typically give 48 hours of their time over a four-week period, but this commitment could waver dramatically according to the severity or regularity of the bombing. For the full-time workers, the *Rescue Service Manual* gives a sense of the enervating demands placed upon human beings in wartime, stating that they had to work 72 hours per week in 12-hour shifts or 84

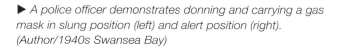

RESCUE SERVICE CREWS – ALLOCATION OF DUTIES

According to the *Rescue Service Manual*, the daily depot programme was broken down into six categories:

OPERATIONAL	To provide that an effective Party or Parties are standing by and ready to go out on duty immediately when called.
DOMESTIC	To allocate the personnel to share in picketing the Depot and lorries, cleaning fatigues, and other domestic duties at the Depot.
TRAINING	To arrange for Parties to undergo Individual Training, Team Training, and Inter-service training.
COMBINED EXERCISES	To provide for Parties to take in Combined Exercises and Mutual Assistance Exercises.
MEALS, ORGANISED RECREATION, AND REST	To allocate appropriate times for meals, organised recreation, physical training, and periods of rest.
WORKS	To detail Parties for such Civil Defence duties as might be allocated.

hours per week in 24-hour shifts. Of course, a portion of these periods would be spent in sleep or at rest, and just on standby, but during the Blitz months rescue crews would find themselves functioning on very little sleep indeed.

EQUIPMENT

The equipment issued to the Rescue Services ranged from basic uniform through to heavy tackle, and was intended to cover all bases in terms of rescue challenge. This being said, the official equipment list was often supplemented by the tools, implements or vehicles that rescuers found practical for the job, based on direct experience.

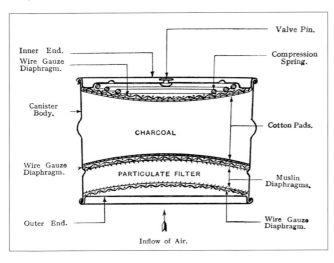

▲ *The filter box of the Civilian Respirator. Gas masks could be useful for rescue workers in keeping out dust, but not leaking coal gas. (Author/Joseph's Militaria)*

▼ *An illustration of the correct routine for Rescue Party equipment inspection drills, taken from the* Rescue Service Manual. *(Author/Joseph's Militaria)*

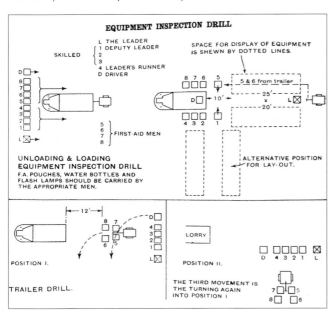

Personal equipment

Each Rescue Service worker was provided as standard with a steel helmet (Service Type, Grade I), the Service Respirator, two sets of protective eyeshields, a serge battledress or blue overall, a greatcoat or waterproof case, a beret (for non-operational duties), a pair of leather boots and a pair of corresponding anklets. When on duty, the man might also receive from unit stocks dust goggles, heavy-duty protective leather gloves, a clasp knife, a small handlamp and a larger electric lamp. Full anti-gas gear was also stored in the depot, including hooded oilskins and anti-gas ointment.

The personal equipment placed an emphasis on protection against dust and smoke, two of the major hazards during a rescue operation. A collapsed building was usually fogged out in a miasma of choking masonry dust and fire smoke, the cloud not only obscuring the view of the scene, but also resulting in watering and painful eyes and respiratory complaints, so strict protective clothing rules had to be observed.

Rescue Party equipment

The rescue equipment issued for each Party included all the manually operated instruments for an immediate rescue. Although it did include equipment that could be used for substantial lifting, it did not contain the mechanisms for major engineering work on scene, such as lifting gear, portable derricks, compressor plant, mechanical excavators and traction engines, and powered bar cutters. These major pieces of equipment were typically in the hands of private companies or works managers, and senior Rescue Services officers were instructed to contact local building contractors and make a list of available equipment, to call on should it be required.

The standard recommended equipment, as given in the official manual, formed an extensive list; the items that are given an asterisk were only provided to the Class B Parties:

- 2 ironshod levers (10ft or 12ft)
- 1 set of tackle blocks, 3-sheave–2 sheave
- *1 30-cwt lifting tackle
- *1 6ft chain (3-ton lift)
- *1 6ft chain (2-ton lift)
- 2 6ft chains (15-cwt lift)
- 1 single-sheave snatch block
- 2 jacks with 10- to 15-ton lift (one only in a Class B Party)
- 1 35ft ladder (extending or two piece)
- *1 100ft length of $^5/_8$in wire rope, with thimbles and shackles
- *2 50ft lengths of $^5/_8$in wire rope, with thimbles and shackles
- 1 100ft length manilla or sisal rope (3in or 4in)
- *1 200ft length manilla or sisal rope (3in or 4in)
- 7 40ft lengths 1½in manilla or sisal lashing lines
- 6 15ft lengths of wire rope (scaffold lashings)
- 2 pairs rubber insulating gloves

► *Soldiers of the Pioneer Corps prepare to break up concrete bomb damage rubble with pneumatic drills. (AirSeaLand Photos)*

- 2 sets remote breathing apparatus (one only in a Class B Party)
- 1 stretcher harness
- 2 sets webbing bands with handles (for carrying casualties)
- 3 pinch bars (or crowbars) with Samson
- 3 sledge hammers, with steel wedges and tongs
- 9 shovels or pointed shovels or blunt-pronged forks
- 3–6 picks or cross mattocks
- 1 heavy axe
- 1 cross-cut saw
- 2 hand saws
- 2 wheelbarrows
- 4 hurricane lamps
- 1 chain saw
- 2–3 short-handled shovels
- 3 scaffold poles (for sheerlegs)
- 3–6 debris baskets or bins
- 6 firemen's axes (with carrying pouches)
- 1 electric inspection lamp with up to 300ft of flex
- 1 short ladder (8–10ft)
- 1 stirrup hand pump with 2 or 3 buckets
- Tarpaulins or stout canvas sheets, or sheets of corrugated iron (to protected trapped persons from falling debris until released)
- 1 fire basket or small electrical bowl fire (for warming trapped persons in winter)
- Box of spikes, timber dogs, etc.
- Timber, deals, blocks for fulcrums for levers etc.
- Supply of puddled clay, for dealing with town gas escapes

Note: 'cwt' refers to 'hundredweight', a measure of weight rarely used in modern Britain, except in some transportation contexts. A measure of 1 cwt equals 112lb or 50.8kg.

In addition to the above, it was recommended that each Party carry with it a 'Box of miscellaneous tools', including a two-edged pruning saw, a bolt cropper, a water stopcock key, a pipe cutter, a slate ripper and an Anderson shelter spanner, the latter a useful piece of kit if the Rescue Party needed to access a smashed-in Anderson shelter. Each party would also carry one first-aid box and two first-aid pouches.

▼*Guidance on how to construct a basic standing derrick, used for winching heavy objects and equipment. (Author/Joseph's Militaria)*

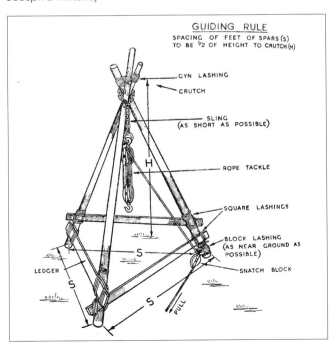

GUIDING RULE
SPACING OF FEET OF SPARS (S)
TO BE ½ OF HEIGHT TO CRUTCH (H)

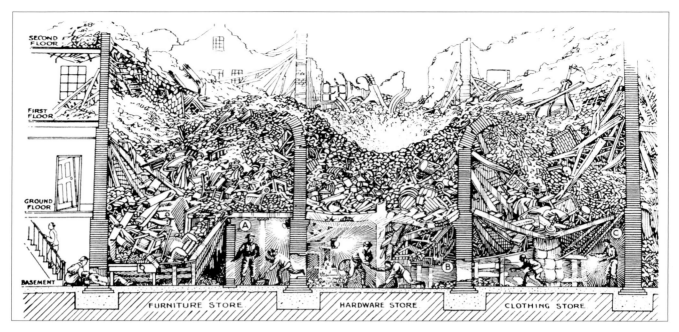

RESCUE PROCEDURES

Actual rescue work required a careful eye and an uninterrupted bias towards caution and safety. Rescue Services personnel were trained, however, to judge the situation not on the level of chaos at the scene – which was almost always profound – but by carefully assessing the urgency required, the type of building involved and the level of damage the building had sustained.

Buildings themselves were placed into two bomb-damage categories. Class 1 buildings were those modern edifices built around a steel or concrete frame; the weight-bearing design of these buildings meant that walls could be demolished by

▼ *A basement rescue where 'the ceiling remains substantially unbroken'. Note how a debris tunnel is constructed over the access point. (Author/Joseph's Militaria)*

▲ *An illustration showing how to effect a basement rescue by breaking through the dividing wall of an adjacent but accessible basement. (Author/Joseph's Militaria)*

the bomb blast, but floors and the roof above might stay intact and stable. Class 2 buildings – the majority of the buildings encountered – carried the weight of the structure on its walls, thus if a wall was destroyed the structure above would often come thundering down. It was noted that Class 1 buildings, if they did collapse, tended to fall down on themselves, creating a relatively localised area of debris, whereas Class 2 buildings might topple and fall some considerable distance from their base. Although the Class 1 buildings were generally safer to work in, rescue workers were cautioned that steel-framed buildings were more susceptible to fire damage than HE damage; although the structure might appear to be holding, fire might progressively weaken steel beams, until the edifice suddenly gave way.

The Blitz taught the Rescue Services some fascinating facts about the way that buildings behaved under bombing. For example, it was noted that wooden floors tended to hold together as a sort of 'raft' during a building collapse, the floorboards and joists falling as a unit, often forming voids beneath in which people might survive. Similarly, ceiling joists would often break in the middle under the sudden rush of tons of weight, but the unbroken portion might hinge downwards from the adjoining wall, forming small angular survival spaces below.

A rescue effort required calm logic on the part of the team leader. The *Rescue Services* manual enjoins the other team members to ask the leader only essential questions and to offer advice only when requested; otherwise they should stay quiet and comply immediately with the directions when given. To bring some method to the scene, the official advice was to respond to the rescue through logical stages:

Stage 1 – Reconnaissance: Conduct a general survey of the damaged building and collect useful information from other individuals (ARP wardens, policemen, neighbours etc.) about the layout of the building, the number of people inside and where they might be hiding. At this stage they also called to and listened for survivors, insisting on as much quiet as possible from those around, as survivors' voices might be both weak from injury and muffled by the debris around them. During the reconnaissance stage, the rescue team evaluated continuing threats, such as gas or water leaks, or unstable walls or floors.

Stage 2 – Immediate rescue: If there were victims in identifiable locations, the rescue team immediately went into action to extract them. This stage might involve some prior actions, such as shoring up destabilised walls, but often it would involve either removing debris to get to the person or, if the debris field was extensive, digging some form of supported shaft down to the victims.

Stage 3 – Exploration: This stage involved searching through 'strong or sheltered parts of the building that are likely to have withstood a blast' for any other survivors, even if there were no clear information about people or their whereabouts. Six specific locations were recommended for exploration:

1. *Specially constructed air raid shelters, inside or outside the building.*
2. *Spaces and cupboards under staircases.*
3. *Basements, cellars, coal holes, etc.*
4. *Points near fire places and chimney breasts.*
5. *Voids and spaces under floors that have not entirely collapsed.*
6. *Rooms which have not been entirely demolished but from which exit is barred by debris.*

The manual advised in the strongest of terms that the rescuers should prioritise the rescue of those *most accessible* first, rather than attempting to reach those in more dangerous and inaccessible circumstances. Time was of the essence during a rescue, and the simple mathematical logic was to bring out as many people as possible, not to effect the most advanced and complicated rescue.

This stage of the rescue might involve first moving on to Stage 4, selected debris removal (see page 119), but it was acknowledged that it was a slow procedure, and the necessities of speed meant that tunnelling might be the quicker option. Tunnelling through tons of precariously

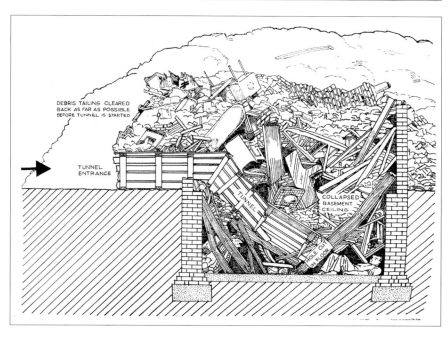

▲ *Constructing debris tunnels was not for the faint-hearted, as tons of pressure might be bearing down on any improvised supports. (Author/Joseph's Militaria)*

unstable debris was not a job for the faint hearted, and required both caution and knowledge. Note that the tunnelling was not exploratory; a tunnel was, as a rule, only dug to reach a precise and known location.

The techniques of tunnelling were akin to those required by a miner, although the *Rescue Services* manual was at pains to point out that 'tunnelling in debris bears little resemblance to engineering tunnelling'. When clearing the passageway, the

▼ *Voids were often formed by collapsing floors, and they formed important survival spaces for home occupants. (Author/Joseph's Militaria)*

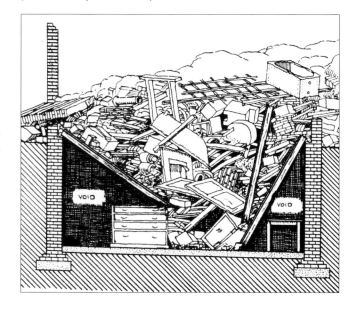

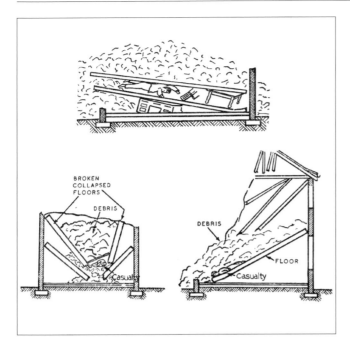

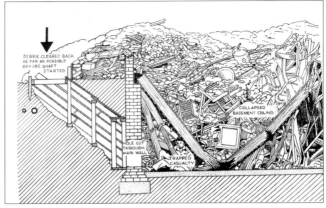

▲ Here we see a ramp cut down through the surrounding soil and debris to reach a casualty trapped in a basement. (Author/Joseph's Militaria)

◄ These three figures show likely voids and spaces to investigate for surviving casualties in collapsed buildings. (Author/Joseph's Militaria)

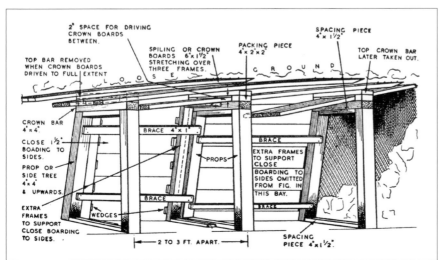

▲ Different frame structures used to create debris tunnels. The supports and framing could be taken from the debris itself or used external building materials. (Author/Joseph's Militaria)

◄ A highly detailed picture of debris tunnel construction. It was important that the tunnel left enough space to bring out the casualty on a stretcher, avoiding making sharp angular turns. (Author/Joseph's Militaria)

rescuers had to be mindful of removing key pieces of rubble that could lead to further collapses. Identifying these pieces was difficult (remember that the rescuers might well be working in conditions of darkness, with strong shadows thrown by artificial lighting), so the safest method of proceeding was to shore up everything. At its most basic, this could involve using simple props with headpieces, the props wedged into position as near vertical as possible, to maximise the load-bearing of the timber. (Timber and other bracing items were generally taken from the surrounding debris field, which typically provided plentiful building materials.) On a more advanced scale, however, tunnels might be constructed with professional scale and sophistication, with fully lined and supported shafts.

Stage 4 – Selected debris removal: This was the most delicate part of the rescue operation, as moving the wrong piece of debris could result in a precipitous further collapse, potentially further entombing or even killing the casualty. It was also important that the rescue team make logical debris removals rather than attempting to sweep away everything in front of them; by targeting certain areas or elements of the debris pile, time and effort could be saved, and the chances of a successful casualty evacuation increased.

There were some key principles informing judicious debris clearance:

1. The team leader should attempt to discover on which floor the victim was supposed to be at the time of the building collapse, and where that floor is lying now.
2. If a floor had collapsed straight down in a horizontal position, it was likely that the victim had gone down with it. Therefore the rescue team should clear as much debris from that floor as possible.
3. When a floor had broken in the centre, and had collapsed in a V shape, it was likely that the victim had slid down to the bottom of the V.
4. If, conversely, a floor had collapsed at one side 'the victim may have slid down and be trapped under the debris at the lower or sagging end of the floor'.
5. Rescue parties should be sensitive to the presence of beds or bedding, as if the casualty was in bed at the time he or she was still likely to be in the vicinity. It was important, however, to search around the bed, as the bomb blast might have thrown the casualty some distance.
6. Debris clearance around chimney breasts and staircases could be profitable, as such architecturally resilient locations might provide survival spaces for the casualties. It was also noted that 'walls whose *edges* face the direction of the blast are usually much less effective than walls that directly face the bomb. Any victims sheltered by such parts of the building may, therefore, be still alive.'

▶ *This illustration shows how to brace a weak wall. The nature of the job illustrates why carpenters were useful members of Rescue Parties. (Author/Joseph's Militaria)*

As much as there was something approaching a science to building rescue operations, the rescue teams in heavily bombed areas soon became soberly realistic about the oddities of explosions and the effects that they had on the victims. One team in London, for example, discovered a woman cradling a baby in the shell of their house, both of them virtually unmarked but nonetheless dead. The husband of the house was discovered behind them, literally embedded into the plaster wall by the force of the explosion. In the *Rescue Service Manual*, crews were told to be mindful of the fact that a direct hit on a building could throw bodies to extreme distances, up to a maximum distance of about 100 yards and the maximum height of about 20 yards. For this reason, the rescue team might have to explore nearby rooftops or open areas for bodies. In instances where the bomb made a crater, bodies were often found at the bottom, 'apparently due to the ease with which a human body will roll down a slope as compared with debris, which tends to stick'. Such unfortunate people tended to be dead, but survivors could sometimes be found buried in the large volumes of earth around the perimeter of the crater.

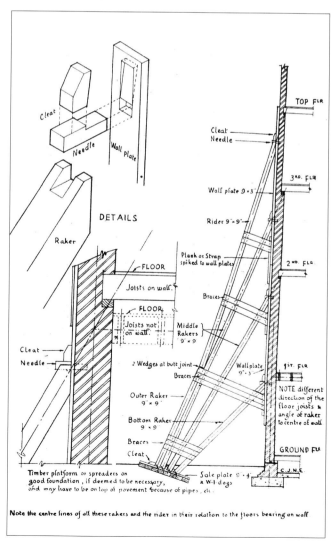

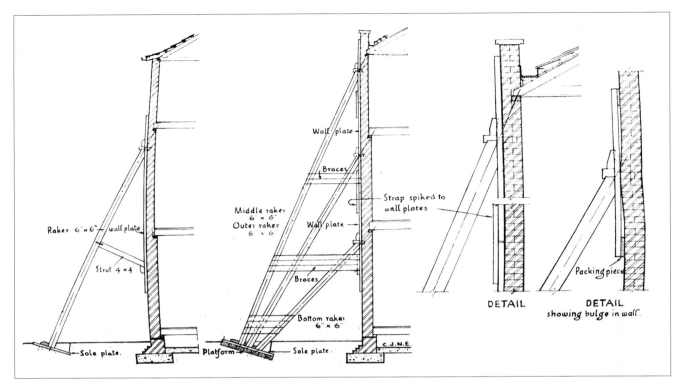

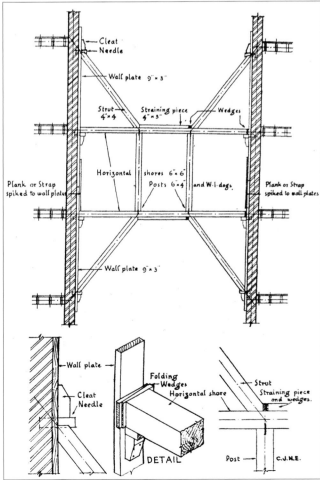

▲ *More wall-shoring instructions. Note that the purpose of shoring was to stop further movement, not push the wall back to its original profile. (Author/Joseph's Militaria)*

◄ *Bracing between damaged walls. Naturally such work was time-consuming, but had to be implemented at great speed to rescue weakening casualties. (Author/Joseph's Militaria)*

▼ *A detailed illustration showing how to shore and brace and bomb-damaged external wall. (Author/Joseph's Militaria)*

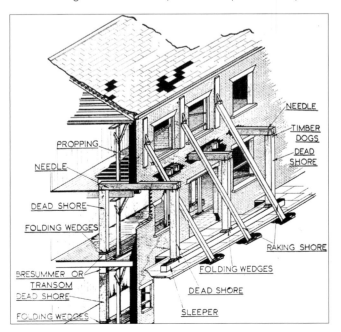

▲ *Bomb damage in a multi-storey building. Although walls and ceilings remain in place, they could suddenly and catastrophically collapse. (Author/Joseph's Militaria)*

Stage 5 – General debris removal: Stage 5 involved the more widespread clearance of debris from the bomb site, when it became apparent that people were still missing, but their location was not known. This stage carried with it elevated risks, as it was likely to result in the disturbance of unstable debris stacks, with the possibility of dangerous collapses. It was also imperative that the rescue teams proceed carefully with the application of their tools, to avoid injuring and killing already vulnerable casualties hidden beneath the rubble. Both human skin and clothing might appear indistinguishable from surrounding masonry when it was heavily impregnated with brick or concrete dust, so care had to be taken to identify what was living and what was not before swinging the pick.

Some of the core rules for debris clearance were as follows:

● Debris should be moved clear of the site if possible, not just moved from one part of the site to the other, or merely 'turned over' and replaced, to avoid confusion about which parts have been searched and which have not. Debris could be shifted physically either in hand-carried debris baskets, wheelbarrows or hoisted baskets for heavier items.
● The team leader needed to allocate specific areas of work for the group of men, to avoid a large crowd gathering and just randomly picking at the rubble. The leader also needed to prevent individuals tramping over unstable sections of debris.

RESCUE EFFORT

The following citation was published in the *London Gazette* on 29 July 1941, explaining the circumstances in which Christopher John Gartland, police sergeant, Herbert Frederick Collier Baker, constable, John Edward Willington Uren, constable, and Thomas Tolen, ARP Rescue Party, were awarded the George Cross for one particular night's work during the Liverpool Blitz:

> *During an air raid a building was demolished by enemy action. Portions of the interior walls collapsed, and the outside wall was leaning dangerously inwards. Gartland, Baker and Uren, accompanied by Tolen, entered the building and, after searching in complete darkness, they found a firewatcher, trapped and almost buried under the debris on the ground floor. When some of the wreckage had been removed, a large wooden beam, which was carrying the weight of the debris of the roof and upper floor and which was directly over the trapped man, appeared about to collapse. Constable Uren at once got under the beam, supporting it with his shoulder. He remained in this position for a considerable time, during which the other three men worked frantically to free the victim. The weight of the beam became too much for Uren to support and Baker took up a position beside him. It was clear that the whole building might collapse at any moment and the Sergeant, who is a man of exceptional strength, placed his arms round the man's body and with a powerful and sustained effort pulled him clear of the debris. Constable Baker then got away from trip beam but owing to the great weight Uren was unable to move. The Sergeant took hold of him and snatched him away bodily. As he did so the upper floor collapsed, completely covering the place where the rescuers had been working. During the whole of this time Tolen had been untiring in his efforts to release the trapped man, entirely regardless of the near danger. Constables Uren and Baker, by supporting the beam for over an hour, made the rescue possible. Had they collapsed under the severe strain, the rescuers and rescued would have been killed. Sergeant Gartland, who was in charge of the operation, showed initiative and leadership of the highest order with complete disregard of danger.*

● Timber would be pulled from the rubble only when it was clear that doing so would not precipitate a further collapse; as already noted, floorboards and joists could form unintended supports, holding up the debris above and forming survival spaces below.
● During the clearance operation, it might have been necessary to put in place timber shoring to prevent further dangerous collapses. Three types of shoring could be applied:

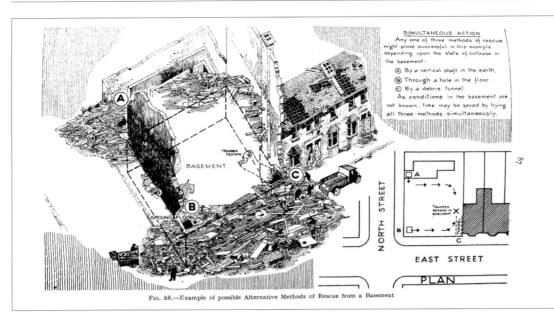

SIMULTANEOUS ACTION
Any one of three methods of rescue might prove successful in this example depending upon the state of collapse in the basement:

(A) By a vertical shaft in the earth.
(B) Through a hole in the floor.
(C) By a debris tunnel

As conditions in the basement are not known, time may be saved by trying all three methods simultaneously.

Fig. 68.—Example of possible Alternative Methods of Rescue from a Basement

◀ *This aerial view shows three options for the rescue of a casualty from a basement. The approach chosen would also be dependent on the size and available equipment of the attending crews. (Author/Joseph's Militaria)*

- Raking shore – used to stop a wall or other vertical structure from toppling or bulging.
- Flying shore – a brace between two facing walls.
- Dead shore – a support holding up the dead weight of a wall or floor.
- If water mains are broken, the water supply needed to

▼ *Rescue workers go into the rubble pile. Note the breathing apparatus pipes being fed to the man at the front, and the tape attached to his arm. (Author/Joseph's Militaria)*

be turned off at the mains outside; the rescuers also had to be mindful of secondary water supplies, such as roof-mounted storage tanks or hot water tanks, and if possible, turn these off as well. Gas leaks were a danger to both casualties and to rescuers; the gas masks used by the rescuers provided no protection from coal gas, plus the gas could explode if mixed with air and brought into contact with a flame. Thus on arrival at the scene of a bombing, no one was allowed to smoke until the presence of gas had been ruled out, or the gas supply safely cut off via the stopcock, which was typically in the basement, near the entrance on the ground floor or under the stairs. If the stopcock couldn't be found or reached, and the escaping gas threatened the casualty, other measures had to be implemented (see feature box).

RESCUE ADVICE – GAS EMERGENCY

From the *Rescue Service* manual:

When the [gas] escape cannot be located or the supply turned off, victims may be saved from asphyxiation by blowing air in large quantities into the lowest accessible part of the debris under which they are trapped. This can best be done with a mobile air compressor, such as is commonly used for road breaking or with other similar apparatus. The air must not be supplied with such force as to stir up dust, of which there is always a considerable quantity in debris, and so add to the existing difficulties. If the end of the air hose is put in a tin can and tied up inside an empty sand bag, this will considerably reduce the blast and give a steadier flow of air.

MEDICAL ASSISTANCE

The British government's pre-war expectations of high casualty levels from enemy bombing led, in the Air Raid Precautions Act 1937 and the Air Raid Precautions (General Schemes) Regulations 1938, to a dramatic expansion of the UK's medical response capability, beyond the regular hospitals, doctors and ambulances that were managed by private concerns or local authorities. (We must remind ourselves that the war was fought in the days prior to the establishment of the National Health Service.) The responsibility for this upscaling was to be borne by the local authorities, who were compelled to a) establish first-aid posts throughout their areas of responsibility; b) acquire the vehicles to deploy mobile first-aid units; and c) recruit and train the personnel who would deliver the medical attention.

In terms of the latter requirement, a wide net was cast. First-aid training was obviously an essential item on the tick list, especially people with a first-aid certification from one of the following organisations:

- St John Ambulance
- St Andrew Ambulance Association
- British Red Cross Society
- London County Council
- National Fire Brigade Association

Nurses and trainee doctors provided another seam of recruitment, as did relevant voluntary and charitable organisations, such as the Joint War Organisation, run by

▼ *Medics and rescue team members practise coordinated mass casualty treatment. Note the majority presence of women among the medics. (AirSeaLand Photos)*

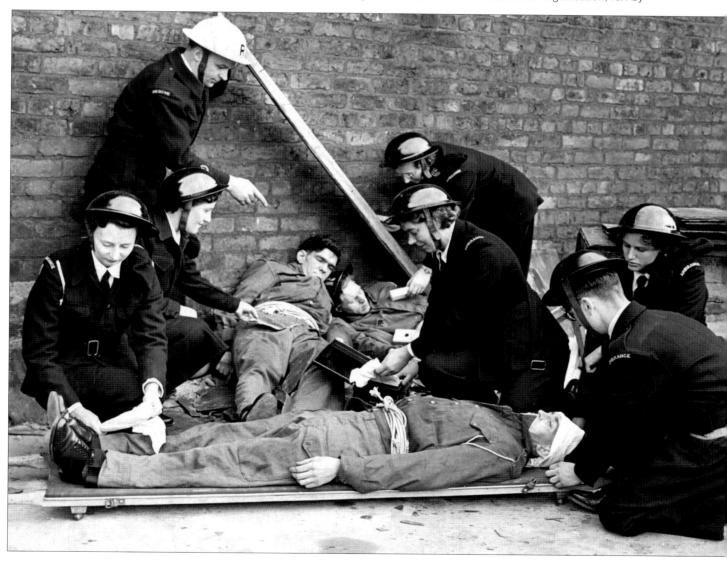

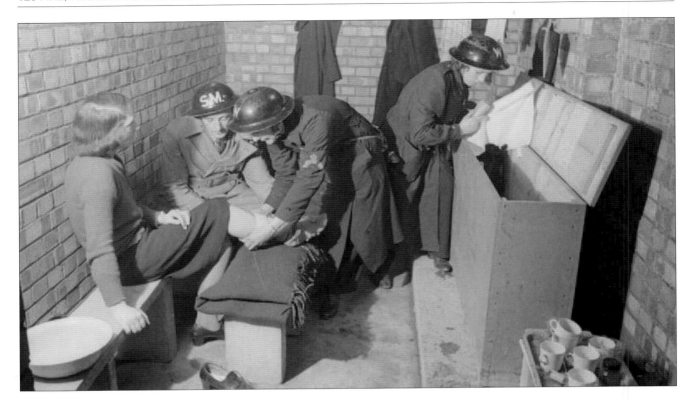

▲ *First Aid area of an air raid shelter in the basement of a London drapery store. An ARP warden checks first aid supplies while two others bandage the ankle of a civilian. (PD)*

rarer as the war progressed. Each outpost would have, ideally, a fully trained doctor and medical team, but naturally there was a limit to what miracles could be performed in an ad hoc treatment centre, thus the seriously injured would be transferred quickly to a hospital, if they hadn't gone there directly in the first place.

As time was of the essence in casualty treatment, Mobile

First Aid Units (MFAUs) were also established. The 1942 government publication *Training in First Aid for Civil Defence Purposes* defined two types of MFAUs:

1. A van containing first-aid personnel and equipment, the people and contents either transported to an emergency location to set up a new first-aid post in a building, or reinforcing the efforts of an overworked fixed post.
2. A 'Light Mobile First Aid Unit', in which a doctor and two or three nurses drove directly to an incident in a light car, with their medical equipment contained in a portable haversack.

▼ *An ARP emergency first aid kit, the partial contents of which are seen top left on the opposite page. (Author/ Joseph's Militaria)*

▼*The Detector, Vapour, Pocket, Mk II was a tin containing a variety of devices for detecting and identifying poison gas. (Author/Joseph's Militaria)*

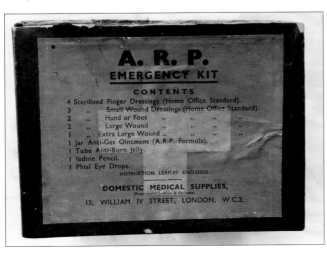

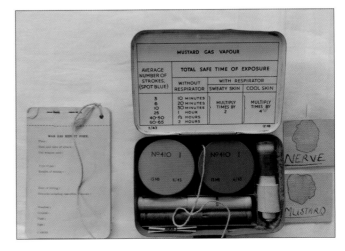

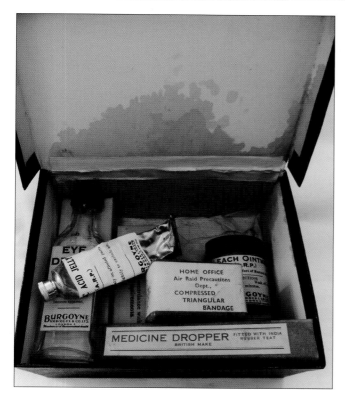

▲ The first aid kit's contents included eye drops, wound dressings, a medicine dropper and a jar of anti-gas ointment. (Author/Joseph's Militaria)

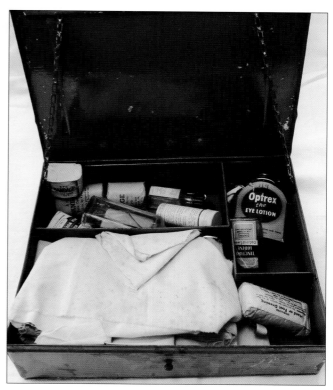

▲ A Boots Minimax ARP medieval kit, which included numerous bandages, a tourniquet and bottles of smelling salts, iodine and picric acid. (Author/Joseph's Militaria)

MEDICAL PROCEDURE

By the end of the Blitz, the British government had a detailed picture of the levels of casualties they could expect in an air raid. The first major raid, on 7 September 1940, produced the rough three-to-one wounded-to-killed casualty ratio (430 dead to 1,600 injured) experienced throughout the Blitz, and this ratio generally persisted throughout the war. Statistical data further clarified that of every 100 air raid casualties:

- 20–25 would be killed
- 20–25 would suffer serious injuries, requiring immediate medical treatments
- the remaining 50–60 would incur slight wounds
- about five or six of those slightly wounded would require hospital treatment

The first step at the scene of a bomb site was naturally to perform triage, assessing the casualties and prioritising them according to the level of medical emergency. Unlike most incidents faced by peacetime medical teams, however, the wartime first-aiders would have to address other pressing concerns simultaneously, including the threat to their own safety from fire, explosions and collapsing buildings. As with the Rescue Parties, a first-aid party would have a designated leader. He would not only oversee and control his team, but he would also report to the Incident Officer (possibly an ARP warden or police

officer), who would have a coordinator responsible for all the teams arriving at the site. The Incident Officer would be identified by an armlet displaying the words 'Incident Officer', or via a blue cloth wrapped around his helmet. For major incidents, the officer might also set up a designated Incident Post, defined by a blue-and-white check flag (a blue flag in London) or at night two blue lamps set one above the other. The Incident Post could be located

▼ This first aid kit was attached to the inside front cover of The Complete First Aid Outfit Book and A.R.P. (Author/ Joseph's Militaria)

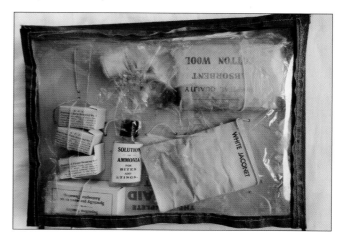

▲ *Two female members of the Indian Ambulance Service. One hundred Indians, including doctors and barristers, joined the unit. During the Blitz, the unit proved itself to be one of the most efficient in Britain. (PD)*

▼ *'Air Raid Precaution Sealing Tape' was used to tape over any structural cracks that might allow poison gas to leak into the home. (Author/Joseph's Militaria)*

anywhere, but often it was situated near the ARP warden's Post, so that the Incident Officer would have convenient access to a telephone.

Once the first-aid team had meaningfully coordinated its efforts with the other agencies, it then focused, according to *Training in First Aid for Civil Defence Purposes*, on three groups of casualties:

1. *those urgently needing attention in order to prevent imminent death, e.g. cases of severe external haemorrhage or of true asphyxia.*
2. *those severely injured and gravely shocked who must have first aid attention in order to make removal possible and to prevent further avoidable shock, which will adversely affect their recovery.*
3. *those who after first aid can make their own way home or to a First Aid Post.*

The manual's guidance also dwelt on the fact that the medics would be operating in exceptional circumstances, with levels of casualty far exceeding even those experienced during most major civil disasters, and more casualties being added with every new wave of bombers. Hence the focus of the medical procedures had to be on a rather blunt efficiency, albeit without losing the caring touch that defined their profession.

For example, it was advised to avoid spending time creating 'elaborate splinting or dressing', instead opting for the simplest solution possible – 'Nothing in the way of first aid beyond the essential should be attempted.' Individuals who were lightly wounded could be asked to walk to hospital under their own steam, leaving cars and ambulances free to take more seriously wounded individuals. If the roads to hospital were blocked, severely wounded casualties would have to be accommodated in the First Aid Post, where they would receive the best treatment possible given the levels of equipment and space there.

Despite the overloading pressures faced by the medical teams, which often involved extreme ethical decisions about who might live or die, they were still urged to exercise compassion and gentle handling of patients. A caring hand on a shoulder or a kind and encouraging word could be the casualty's first step to psychological as well as physical recovery.

One of the most unpalatable aspects of life in the Civil Defence services was the close-up encounter with the dead, in various states of mutilation. This could be the stuff of nightmares. Rescuers sometimes had to try to assemble body parts into 'whole' corpses, but were frustrated by finding imbalanced numbers of limbs to torsos, or finding the right number but noting that they had an excess of left or right legs. They might find themselves having to clean up large numbers of dead for identification, sometimes doing so with crude slaps of a wet mop because of time pressures. The experience of encountering the dead could be life-changing, as suggested here in the account of Irene

A broom used as a thigh splint by placing the handle along the injured limb, with the head of the broom at the feet. Loosely folded pieces of newspaper or other material may be used as padding, placed between the ankle and knee joints, and also at the hip.

Folded triangular bandages are shown in the illustration, but the improvised splint may be secured by any other material of sufficient length, such as, for example, neck-ties, belts, or scarves.

▲ *A medical illustration showing how to immobilise a casualty with a fractured femur, ready for safe transportation to a hospital. (Author/Joseph's Militaria)*

Haslewood, a driver for a stretcher-bearer party who was called to Sloane Square tube station after it took a direct hit on 19 November 1940, hitting a train just as it was leaving the station:

I believe the utter carnage of the disaster beggared description. Some of the men who had been working on the job tried to tell me about it. They hardly got anyone out alive. Most of the poor bodies had been stripped of their clothing from the blast. Two stark naked and mutilated girls hung high up in the twisted steel girders – trapped by their feet hanging downwards. The men could not get them released for days, and had to work under this ghastly spectacle. They never found out how many dead they collected, because there were so many small bits and pieces of bodies they could not reckon things out. The men collected these gruesome pieces in dustpans – and then of course the question arose of what to do with them? They did not know whether to send them to the mortuary or to Durhams Wharf – where all the refuse is taken away in barges down the river. I am glad to say that they decided on the latter.' (Quoted in Gardiner 2010, n.p.)

In official instruction, of course, the depth of the horrors was not spelled out, but there was dark and realistic advice. Ideally, a doctor had to confirm that a person was dead, unless the mutilation was so severe the fact was obvious. If a doctor wasn't available, a fully qualified first-aider could certify. Once death was confirmed, the details of the body had to be logged on an official form:

1. Address where recovered.
2. Location of the body within the building.
3. Time and date when the body was recovered.
4. The apparent cause of death.
5. A signature of a responsible person, such as a Rescue Party Leader.
6. Any other information that might clarify the person's identity.

Beyond that, there was nothing more to be done for the casualty. To balance out those who were lost, however, Britain's wartime emergency services also had the flush of satisfaction that came from a successful rescue, or a life saved, of which there were thankfully many thousands.

▼ *Stabilisation of a fractured arm using a newspaper. The sheer volume of casualties meant improvisation was often required. (Author/Joseph's Militaria)*

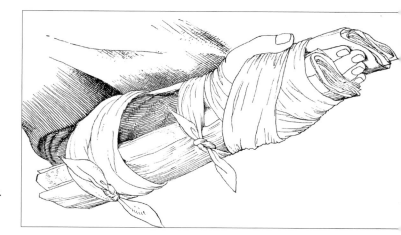

CHAPTER SIX

LIFE UNDER THE BLITZ

The Blitz experience depended very much on where you lived in the UK. Out in rural provincial Britain, you might have been forgiven for forgetting, at times, that there was a war on. In inner-city industrial areas, by contrast, the Blitz brought maximum disruption to every act of living, including the imminent threat of death, critical injury or homelessness. The island nation very much had to adapt and survive.

In this chapter, we will delve into some of the accommodations that the British people had to make during the Blitz. Note that this is not an exploration of the home front per se, but rather of the direct effects of the Blitz and air raid precautions, from the blackout to post-raid procedures.

◄ *Firefighters lean in to the pressure of their hose. During the first 22 days of the Blitz, UK firefighters combatted more than 10,000 individual fires, including massive industrial blazes. (Shutterstock)*

BLACKOUT

Although electronic navigational aids were available to the Luftwaffe during World War II (as we saw in Chapter 2), and were of increasing sophistication as the war progressed, visual navigation and eyesight target acquisition were still of central importance to both the ability of an air fleet to arrive at the right target and to put its bombs even roughly within the target area. Certain navigational features could scarcely be obscured, such as coastlines and major rivers, especially on moonlit nights. (The Thames was especially inconvenient, snaking as it did through the industrial heartlands and docks of London.) But artificial illumination could be controlled. Domestic, transport and industrial lighting were all, under the right conditions, visible at even medium–high altitudes.

▼ *In an effort to be visible to cars and other pedestrians, this stylish couple have attached strips of white paper to their clothes. (Getty/Fox Photos)*

Cognisant of this fact, on 2 September 1940 the office of the Lord Privy Seal (who was at this time John Anderson, 1st Viscount Waverley, replaced shortly afterwards by Samuel Hoare), published the following announcement to the nation:

A lighting order has been made under Defence Regulation No. 24 and comes into operation at sunset tonight as a further measure of precaution. The effect of the order is that every night from sunset to sunrise all lights inside the buildings must be obscured and lights outside buildings must be extinguished, subject to certain exceptions in the case of external lighting where it is essential for the conduct of work of vital national importance. Such lights must be adequately shaded.

This was the origin of the 'blackout', a lengthy period in which night-time Britain attempted to obscure itself from aerial view.

HOUSEHOLD AND COMMERCIAL BLACKOUT

For householders, the chief measure of the blackout was to prevent light escaping from windows and through glass-fronted doors, indeed any aperture. For windows, the chief measure was to hang thick blackout curtains, extending the drop either side of the window frame. Windows could also be boarded up, or thick card or multiple sheets of paper taped across the window frame. Another alternative was to paint the glass with a heavy bitumastic or oil 'blackout paint'; in British newspapers from 1945, there are numerous advertisements offering the products or services to remove such a tenacious substance.

External doors presented something of an additional challenge, for while closed they obstructed light, but let it flood out when opened. This problem was largely negotiated through good practice – the householder needed to ensure that internal lights were turned off before opening a door on to the street. For commercial premises that were heavily frequented, particularly shops, the problem was more acute, owing to the front door opening and closing often. The solution here was either to close the shop before darkness set in or to fashion an entry system that prevented light escape, such as two spaced blackout curtains behind the door (the customer would step into the darkened space, closing the first curtain behind them, then opening the second curtain) acting like an air-lock but for light.

For larger industrial units, the blackout brought a major change in the internal ambience. Some premises had glass roofs to permit maximum natural light on the assembly line, and once these were obscured troglodyte conditions prevailed on the factory floor, with the workers having to labour under harsh artificial light even in the daytime. (The blackout installation had to remain up during the day, being too labour-intensive to install and remove on a daily basis.)

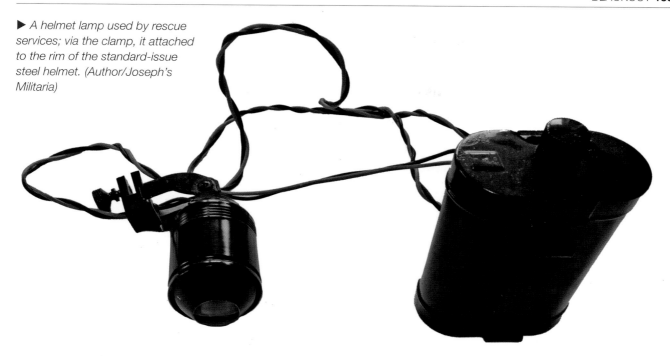

▶ A helmet lamp used by rescue services; via the clamp, it attached to the rim of the standard-issue steel helmet. (Author/Joseph's Militaria)

There were also issues regarding ventilation; as windows now largely had to remain closed, natural air sources were often restricted. There were some cultural effects too – gone were the days of brightly lit or neon signs glowing warmly outside cinemas and theatres.

STREETS AND TRAFFIC

The blackout measures were also vigorously enforced outside homes. All street lighting was turned off, and for a time it was considered an offence to light a match or smoke outside, even though the chances of a Luftwaffe bomber crewman at 18,000ft spotting a briefly glowing cigarette were almost non-existent. Torches were at first not permitted, although this regulation was later relaxed when the lethal impact of the Blitz became felt – some torches (especially the No. 8 pocket

torch) could be used as long as they were dimmed with screening of tissue paper and the beam was kept pointed at the ground. Citizens could also purchase commercial models of blackout lamps, which featured either a prominent hood or a rotating shade device.

One of the biggest impacts of the blackout was on transportation. Mindful that vehicles were still going to have to move upon Britain's roads, vehicle lighting was still permitted, but with severe modifications that reduced the light emitted to an unhelpful glow rather than a guiding beam (see overleaf). At first, only sidelights were permitted, but then it was allowed to use one headlamp fitted with a slit-type light reducer. Interior lights were not permitted, nor were reversing lights, and rear lights and brake lights had to be light-reduced.

The transportation blackout also affected trains and other public vehicles, and the stations from which they left. Bulbs aboard trains, for example, had to be painted blue, or were extinguished altogether during air raids. The passengers therefore had to feel their way through pitch-black compartments.

◀ Britain's civil defence effort extended to the Commonwealth. This poster is from Australia, where air raids were seen as a real threat, and was designed to reinforce the message that blackout regulations were a matter of life and death. (PD)

▶ This ARP blackout lamp has an upper shield to keep the beam of light reflected downward at the ground, reducing the risk of being spotted by aircraft. (Author/Joseph's Militaria)

BLACKOUT MEASURES – CARS AND BICYCLES

Upon announcement of the blackout on 2 September 1939, it was obligatory for car owners to fit their vehicles with light-reducing measures, and to black out completely many of their lights. Recognising that the population had little time to implement these measures, the Lighting Restriction Order gave vehicle owners permission to use the following modifications, albeit for one night only:

- Headlamps – A thick disc of cardboard inserted behind the lamp glass, with a semicircular hole cut into the centre (although not above the centreline of the lamp bulb). The hole could not be more than 2in wide, and the straight side of the semicircle had to be uppermost.
- Sidelamps – These had to be covered with two thicknesses of newspaper, and side, rear and top panels had to be totally obscured.
- Rear lamps – Every rear lamp apart from the red rear lamps and amber stop lights had to be completely obscured; exposed lamps were to be dimmed with two thicknesses of newspaper.

▲ *A poster common during the blackout era explains to motorists each point regarding how a car's illumination had to be limited. Driving at night became a strained experience, and only if essential. (Author/1940s Swansea Bay)*

For cyclists, the restrictions were (according to the *Daily Telegraph* newspaper published on 2 September 1939):

The upper half of the front glass must be completely obscured;
The lower half of any reflector must be treated with black paint or otherwise rendered non-effective;
Panels or windows provided for the emission of light other than that facing to the front must be completely obscured;
All other apertures such as those provided for ventilation must as far as practicable be screened to prevent the emission of light, particularly in an upward direction;
The light emitted by the lamp must be white.

▶ *This battery-powered electric lamp had a blackout hood and a rotating lens fitting for red or clear light emission. (Author/Joseph's Militaria)*

BLACKOUT EFFECTS

The blackout regulations were rigorously enforced by ARP wardens and police, sometimes with pedantic absurdity. There were cases of people receiving heavy fines for the most insignificant or fleeting levels of light emission. In November 1940, for example, a serving officer in the Naval Reserve in Yarmouth received a fine for striking a match so that his female companion could actually see the dial in a telephone box. Such intolerant policing, or the stentorian shout to 'Get that light out!', instantly made the blackout sit awkwardly with the largely tolerant British.

But beyond that, the effects of the blackout on the population's safety were profound. Pedestrians were constantly being injured from a range of night-time accidents – falling from unseen steps or kerbs, walking into walls or posts, dropping into ditches or roadworks. Passengers stepping to or from trains were especially vulnerable, as both trains and stations were often blacked out, making it all too easy to fall off a platform or between the platform and the train. One man even stepped from a train in Denham, Buckinghamshire, and fell 80ft, not realising that the (temporary) stop point was a viaduct, and not a station.

Pedestrians were also regularly hit by cars, and vehicle accidents reached crisis levels. In 1940, 9,169 people died in road accidents, which equated to one death per 200 vehicles on the road; today's figure is about one death per 20,000 vehicles on the road. There was also a rise in industrial accidents, along with a host of physical complaints due to working in low-light conditions. On 29 November 1939, for example, the *Newcastle Evening Chronicle* reported that 1,400 drivers and conductors on public transport in the north-east of England had complained of 'eye-strain headache', from straining to see information on tickets or driving controls. There could be worse consequences. Blackout conditions were a contributory factor in several major train accidents, including that at Eccles on 30 December 1941, which killed 23 people and injured a further 57.

There was also some level of chaos in just getting about. Pedestrians became lost in familiar cities rendered alien by absolute darkness. Train passengers frequently got off at the wrong station. Car drivers made numerous wrong turns, unable to see road signs even just a few feet away. The blackout also aided a significant surge in levels of crime, especially thefts (often related to looting of bombed-out buildings), assaults and even murders, as we saw in Chapter 4.

The British government and local authorities began to respond to the problems created by the blackout. Partly, their

▶ *A blackout visor for fitting to vehicle headlights. Once these were in place, the light projected from the vehicle would be very dim indeed. (Author/Joseph's Militaria)*

first port of call was to provide advice, typically distributed through leaflets and newspapers. A typically cautionary advert was published in the *Buckinghamshire Herald*, 2 February 1940:

WAIT!
YOU CAN SEE THE CAR – WHEN THE DRIVER *CAN'T SEE YOU!*
Four simple rules for getting home safely in the black-out:

1. *When you first come out into the black-out, stand still for a minute to get your eyes used to the darkness.*
2. *Look both ways before stepping off the pavement. Make sure there's nothing coming.*
3. *Where there are traffic lights, always cross by them. It is worth going out of your way to do this.*
4. *Throw the light of your torch down onto the ground.*

But there were also more practical general measures introduced. A 20mph speed limit was imposed on drivers, reducing the risk of collision with a pedestrian and the likelihood of very serious injury if it did occur. White lines were painted on kerbs, steps and on/around other potential hazards at ground level. White hazard lines were also painted down the centre of roads to help prevent head-on collisions; these are still very much a part of British road markings today. Again for pedestrians, luminous armbands became available to make them more 'spottable' in the dark. Some measures were a little less conventional: citizens were encouraged to eat plenty of carrots to improve their eyesight; there is some scientific basis to this practice, but under such severe dark conditions the payoffs were minimal.

Eventually, beyond the Blitz, the blackout became what has been referred to as a 'dim-out'. Street illumination came back on, albeit of very low power – about one-third of the strength allowed in pre-war 1939. Theatres and cafes were allowed to relight their neon signs. When the air raid sirens did sound, however, all citizens and premises had to revert immediately to full blackout procedure.

◄ *The blackout brought with it a whole new world of considerations. Here Dettol antiseptic is promoted as safe for application in dark conditions. (Author/Joseph's Militaria)*

▼ *These sophisticated blackout curtains include ventilated sections, hopefully to prevent the room becoming stale when sealed up. (Getty/Hulton Deutsch)*

It can be used in the dark

The first thing asked of an antiseptic is that it shall kill germs. But that is not enough. In darkness or emergency there may be neither time nor opportunity for precise diluting. The antiseptic must be used promptly and freely if septic infection is to be avoided. If, then, there is risk of corrosion or poisoning *by the antiseptic itself,* quick action may well do more harm than good.

The marked superiority of 'Dettol', the modern antiseptic, is that, though deadly to germs, it is kind to human tissue. Though *three times more efficient* germicidally than pure carbolic acid, it is entirely non-poisonous, and may be used safely, if necessary at full strength. It is clean and pleasant: it does not even stain. 'Dettol' in First Aid is simply invaluable. It can be used in the dark.

DETTOL
THE MODERN ANTISEPTIC
TRADE MARK

THE GAS THREAT

If we were to choose a single object representing the Blitz era in Britain, the gas mask would arguably be the one. This is ironic, as of all the threats that materialised over the British Isles during World War II, poisonous gas was not one of them, regardless of how much it was feared. And yet, gas masks were a standard household object for the Blitz generation.

The logic for fearing gas was that as gas weapons had been a prominent feature of warfare in World War I it seemed almost inconceivable that such weapons would not be used in strategic bombing campaigns. Indeed, the 1930s had seen the use of air-dropped chemical weapons in earnest; the Italian Air Force had dropped chemical ordnance on Ethiopian tribesmen during the 1935–36 Italo-Ethiopian War, specifically the blister agent sulphur mustard and the vomiting agent diphenylchloroarsine. British officials envisaged that gas would maximise the horror of conventional weapons, e.g. mustard gas would be deployed (either via bombs or by direct spraying) in conjunction with HE bombs, the explosives causing the intense material damage while the mustard gas prevented the rescue and fire crews from performing their Civil Defence responses effectively. Thus in 1938, as fears of German strategic bombing intensified, the British government began the large-scale production of gas masks for every man, woman and child in the UK. By September 1939, some 38 million had been distributed. Every ARP warden and Civil Defence worker would go about their business with a gas-mask container banging against his or her hip. Schoolchildren would carry them to school and store them under their desks during lessons, only bringing them out for air raid drills. They became one of the most ubiquitous items distributed throughout wartime Britain.

▲ The cleanliness and space of this imagined garden dug-out is conspicuous. Note the air trap section below the overhead entrance. (Author)

The major government publication defining responses to gas attack was *Air Raid Precautions Handbook No. 1: Personal Protection Against Gas*, which ran to 124 pages and was already in its second edition by the onset of war. In its first few pages, it listed the four categories of gas/ chemical threat, and the specific gases within each category. These were:

a) *Tear gas*. – Any eye irritant which even in very small amounts has an immediate effect upon the eyes, causing intense smarting, a profuse flow of tears and spasm of the eyelids, which generally make it very difficult to see. In pure air the effects of the vapour soon pass off, and no damage is caused to the eyes though the *liquid* of persistent tear gas *may* cause permanent injury to the eye.

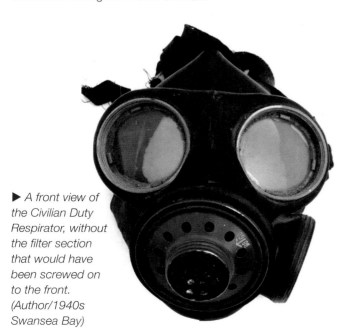

▶ A front view of the Civilian Duty Respirator, without the filter section that would have been screwed on to the front. (Author/1940s Swansea Bay)

▶ The inside of the Civilian Duty Respirator. This is the CD Mk I model, with a gas container made of waterproofed carboard. (Author/1940s Swansea Bay)

◄ *An ARP warden in full protective clothing here swabs the ground with a detector stick, seeking to identify the presence and type of gas. (Author).*

▶ *Gas mask boxes were utilitarian in appearance, so many women covered them in cloth to make them more decorative. (Author/1940s Swansea Bay)*

These gases are often called 'lachrymators.'

b) *Nose irritant gas.* – Irritant smoke produced from certain arsenical compounds are in this class, but though they produce intense pain in the nose, throat and breathing passages during exposure to the gas, these painful effects soon pass off in fresh air.

c) *Lung irritant gas.* – An irritant gas which attacks the breathing passages and lungs. Chlorene and phosgene are examples of this type, and will produce death if breathed in sufficiently large quantities.

The gases are sometimes called 'choking gases'.

d) *Blister gases.* – These substances, of which mustard gas is a typical example, cause intense irritation or burning of the skin according to the amount of gas which has come into contact with the affected part. In severe cases deep and extensive blisters may be caused.

These gases are known as 'vessicants'.

▼ *An army sergeant adjusting and explaining gas masks to Welshpool ARP wardens. The van in the background was a testing chamber for the masks. (PD)*

Personal Protection Against Gas provided guidance for the average citizen and ARP personnel about what signs and symptoms to look for to indicate a poison attack. Thus tear gas would inflict an immediate eye-watering effect, the first sign of phosgene gas might be 'a pronounced smell of musty hay', while mustard gas 'has a faint but characteristic smell suggestive of horseradish, onions or garlic'.

In terms of official public warning, the local ARP warden would be issued with a 'gas rattle', essentially a classic rotary wooden football rattle, used to alert local houses to the presence of the noxious chemicals. There was also the use of chemical detector sprays and paints, of greenish-yellow colour, but which would turn red if they came into contact with liquid blister agents. These paints were applied to publicly visible objects, such as telephone boxes or police boxes.

TYPES OF GAS MASK

Apart from those used for babies (described below), the gas masks issued during war were designed mainly to protect the face, eyes and lungs, not the skin. The wearer was cautioned to be cognisant of the fact that while the masks might shield the wearer against weaponised gases, they did not protect against common household or industrial gases, such as carbon monoxide, exhaust gas and petrol vapour.

The key types of gas mask were as follows:

The Civilian Respirator

The most common and historically familiar of the gas mask types, the Civilian Respirator had a rubber facepiece, fitted with a single 'window'-type visor, that enclosed the entire face and sides of the head, held in place by three straps that met in a buckle at the back of the head. Each strap was adjustable to ensure a close, tight fit, and safety pins provided on each strap were used to pin the final position in place so that it wouldn't be inadvertently altered. The respirator filter cylinder (the G.C. Mark II) was attached to the nosepiece of the mask via a strong rubber band (these rubber bands became very popular among small boys as catapult elastic during the late war and post-war years). It contained two filter sections, one a particulate filter to prevent 'the passage of finely divided smokes like the arsenical gases' plus a larger

▲ *The Civilian Respirator correctly fitted. This type of respirator was the most common issued to the general population of the UK. (Author)*

▶ *A Civilian Respirator with its original box. Instructions advised the owner to keep the mask away from damp, strong light and chemicals. (Author/1940s Swansea Bay)*

filter of activated charcoal that absorbed phosgene and mustard gases. As well as a chemical filter, the respirator had a one-way valve that closed on breathing out, 'thus preventing air being passed back through the container'. (It is important to note that the particulate filters of the Civilian Respirator and many other gas masks contained both crocidolite – otherwise known as 'blue asbestos' – and arsenic. Although they were harmless in their solid state, the subsequent passage of time has resulted in these filters breaking down in antique masks, presenting a serious health hazard if worn and used without the filters being removed

professionally first.) The Civilian Respirator was supplied in a strong cardboard box featuring instructions on the lid. Incidentally, given the fact that respirators accompanied people everywhere, many women covered the boxes with decorative fabric, in an effort to inject a little fashion into wartime austerity.

Civilian Duty Respirator

The Civilian Duty Respirator (CDR) was similar in principle to the Civilian Respirator, but with a more robust quality of construction for issue to Civil Defence and other ARP workers. The rubber was of a

▶ *Clad in protective oilskin and rubber clothing, this decontamination squad was trained by the Corporation of the City of London specifically to deal with gas attacks, which thankfully never came. (Keystone/Getty Images)*

▲ *A Civilian Service Respirator. The eyepieces of this respirator were made of splinterless glass, an essential property for workers in harm's way. (Author/1940s Swansea Bay)*

▼ *A diagram of the Civiilian Service Respirator. The image top right is the connector between the breathing valve and the main tube. (Author)*

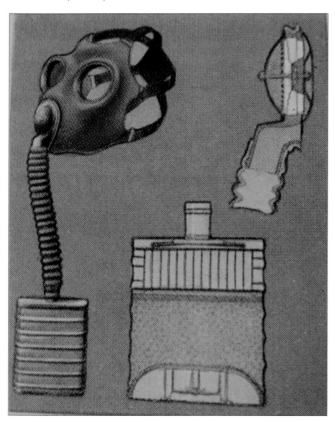

heavier standard and the design fitted more closely to the face, plus there were additional fittings: an outlet valve and a fitting on the left cheek to accept a microphone. Instead of the one-piece window visor, the CDR had two separate eyepieces consisting of glass panels, which could be individually unscrewed from the metal rims for cleaning. In some models, the glass also came with a gelatin coating that prevented fogging and dimming. If this was not fitted, the CDR came with an anti-dimming compound and cloth; with the compound evenly applied using the finger, and spread evenly using the cloth, any moisture build-up on the glass would be dispersed evenly in a film through which the wearer could still see. (On the standard Civilian Respirator, it was recommended to achieve a similar effect by applying a thin film of toilet soap using a wetted finger.)

Civilian Service Respirator

The Civilian Service Respirator was quite different in appearance to the previous respirators mentioned, in that its filter container was housed separately from the face mask, connected to the mask by a long flexible hose. This mask was an armed services type, and could withstand longer exposure to gas, and allowed greater freedom of movement, as the heavy container was carried by the chest, and not by the face. Thus this gas mask tended to be seen only in the possession of Civil Defence workers. The container itself was issued in several different types, labelled by the letters A, D and E, the principal difference between the types being the point at which air was drawn into the container and the way in which the internal filtering contents were arranged (like the other containers, this gas mask contained a large section of activated charcoal plus a particulate filter). The Type A, however, was only intended for training purposes.

Baby Respirator

The rather terrifying-looking respirator for babies almost entirely encased the infant in a rubberised canvas suit, worn much like a nappy but with only the legs free. The baby would look at its parent through the large visor at the front. The baby's mask differed from the others not just in appearance; the asbestos filter for the mask was attached to the side, and attached to that was a concertina hose with a handle. The handle was pumped back and forth, the operator actively drawing the air into the mask space. Of course, the implication of this procedure was that if the operator stopped pumping, for whatever reason, the infant would ultimately be deprived of air; there are indeed reports of babies going somewhat limp through parental inattention.

Gas masks were an omnipresent aspect of British life during the Blitz, even if they were not used to counter the threat for which they were devised. Schools, offices and commercial premises would conduct regular drills and it was a legal requirement to have a gas mask accessible at all times. For Britain's citizens, however, it was bombs that constituted the real threat, and for that they headed down into the shelters.

▲ This view of the baby respirator clearly shows the air pump on the side, through which filtered air was pumped inside the mask. (Author/1940s Swansea Bay)

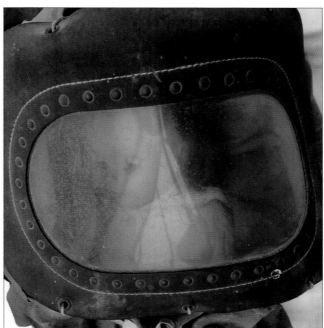

▲ The visor of the baby respirator gave a clear view of the infant, but did little to alleviate the sense of claustrophobia inside. (Author/1940s Swansea Bay)

▼ The rear frame of the baby respirator. The filter on the side (here the right side) was an asbestos type and canvas parts were rubber-coated. (Author/1940s Swansea Bay)

▼ Breathing apparatus used in rescue work had to provide protection from smoke inhalation while also offering good all-round visibility. (Author/1940s Swansea Bay)

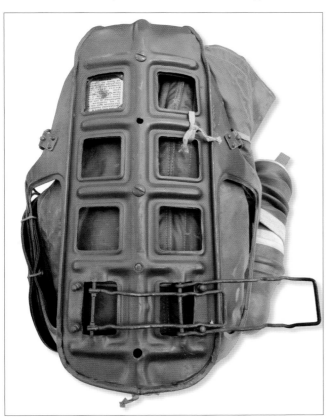

LIFE IN THE SHELTERS

Although many towns and cities in Britain received heavy bombing during the Blitz months, the majority of Britain's population lost neither property nor persons during the war. What most experienced, however, were the seemingly endless cold, damp nights in the shelters.

CONDITIONS

During the dark days of the Blitz, and especially in the first months of the experience, public shelter provision was haphazard and inconsistent. Many shelters in the bomb-hit areas had no lights, lavatories and even seating, or else one or two chemical toilets might be provided for several hundred people; these quickly overflowed and contributed to the noisome atmosphere created by inadequate ventilation. People slept and sat directly on hard concrete floors, enduring sleepless nights, or they brought a cluttered accumulation of deck chairs, mattresses, cushions and other slight home comforts.

One of the worst of these improvised shelters was the Tilbury shelter off Commercial Road in London, basically a semi-underground goods storage/terminal area of Liverpool Street station. Although a specific area had been marked off for the occupation of c. 3,000 people, during the raids the capacity swelled uncontrollably to more than 10,000 people, according to journalist estimates, the excess flowing into areas that did not have official shelter status. Journalist Ritchie Calder, writing for the *Daily Herald*, famously captured the grim conditions inside:

> [the shelter] was not only the most unhygienic place I have ever seen, it was [. . .] definitely unsafe [. . .] yet numbers as high, on some estimates, as 14,000 to 16,000 people crowded into it on those dreadful nights when hell was let loose on East London.* [. . .] People of every type and condition, every colour and creed, found their way there. [. . .] Scotland Yard knew where to look for criminals bombed out of Hell's Kitchen. Prostitutes paraded there. Hawkers peddled greasy, cold fried fish which cloyed the already foul atmosphere. Free fights had to be broken up by the police. Couples courted. Children slept. Soldiers, sailors and airmen spent part of their leave there.

*We now know these to be exaggerated figures, although the claustrophobia of the situation is not to be doubted.

Calder's image of shelter life was harrowing. He described how people waded 'ankle deep in filth', or 'slept in the dust

◄ *Aldwych Underground station her serves as an air raid shelter. The branch and station were actually closed from September 1940 until 1946. (AirSeaLand Photos)*

between the rails and on the cobblestone of the railway'. Things became so bad that there were even cases of what we might term 'war tourism'; Londoners from safer or better-off parts of the city headed down to Tilbury to take in the sights. Eventually, nearby commercial premises were repurposed as shelters, which released some of the human pressure inside Tilbury, but the shelter remained a grim refuge throughout the Blitz.

Shelter governance was also a significant issue. Most public shelters had 'shelter marshals', individuals given the onerous responsibility of overseeing order and sanitation within the shelter. Many of these individuals had little in the way of official authority, and therefore relied largely upon personal strength and charisma to control the masses. They would also be assisted by a variety of voluntary organisations, whose work inside the shelters often made all the difference between a semblance of order and outright chaos.

The personal behaviour of people in relation to the shelters did not always help matters. As Calder highlights in his reporting, public shelters could be magnets for criminals and criminality. The wartime newspaper archives hold hundreds of articles that include the words '… was arrested in an air raid shelter'. There were problems of people using the shelters excessively – i.e. when no air raid was occurring – either because they had been bombed out of their own home or for a host of other personal and even social reasons. Excessive use of shelters, and even acts of intended or careless vandalism, could bring blunt responses from the local authorities. A notice in the *Western Daily Press* on 1 June 1940 stated that 'Considerable wanton damage is being done to public air raid shelters. Those at Wedmore Vale, Melvin Square, Bedminster Down and Eastville Park were so badly damaged on Thursday night that they would have been ineffective and dangerous had a raid occurred that night.' The notice ended with an exhortation that 'The public has no right to enter a shelter except during a raid and YOU CAN HELP by pointing this out to anyone (including children) attempting to enter.'

PUBLIC HEALTH

A further problem with the public shelters was health related. The crowded shelters, often in the poorer neighbourhoods, were near-perfect environments for the transmission of communicable diseases – the common cold, sore throats and flu were spread easily in the damp, warm and thick air, and also by the practice of people shaking out bedding in the morning. Notices in shelters advised people against this, telling them to take bedding home before shaking it out, and also spread the message to carry and use a handkerchief, under the famous strapline 'Coughs and sneezes spread diseases'. The biggest concern to the government,

▲ *Two elderly ladies seek to make themselves comfortable in the crypt of Christ Church in Spitalfields, London, in November 1940. (AirSeaLand Photos)*

however, was that the country's city populations would be laid low with an epidemic of measles, diphtheria or whooping cough. Thankfully, this did not happen.

SHELTER ADVICE

There was no shortage of public advice about how to cope in the shelters both mentally and physically. One popular volume of shelter and Blitz wisdom was *A.R.P. at Home: Hints for Housewives*, published by the Ministry of Home Security in 1941 and written by a Mrs Creswick Atkinson, the Welfare Advisor in London Regional Headquarters. The focus on a female readership for this booklet was pertinent. During

the Blitz, hundreds of thousands of men were conscripted into the armed forces and sent either to UK barracks or deployed overseas, or took on roles in Civil Defence, thereby committing them to frequent night duties. The women left at home, therefore, frequently had to cope with air raids and shelter life on their own, often while looking after dependent children.

The first pages of *A.R.P. at Home: Hints for Housewives* are devoted to ensuring that shelters were properly located and constructed (see Chapter 1). Subsequent instruction, however, focuses upon how to implement good practice and organised thinking to make the shelter experience more bearable. The following are some of the key elements of advice, based on the original text.

Before you go to the shelter

- Pack a bag with a complete change of clothing and leave it with a friend who lives in another part of town. This means you will have some back-up clothes in case you cannot immediately return home following the raid.
- Place any valuables or important documents (insurance policies, deeds etc.) in a safe place, and if such a place can't be found then take the items with you into the shelter.
- Avoid taking large sums of money with you into the shelter. Atkinson's advice: 'The best thing to do it put all spare money into National Savings. It will be safe there and you can easily get it if you need to.'
- Before leaving your house, draw back all curtains and blinds; this enables you to see at a glance if a fire has started inside.
- Turn off all gas taps and the gas at the mains. Also shut down any pilot light and mains electricity.

◀ *This scene from a shelter in the West End of London illustrates the enforced physical and social intimacy of shelter life during the Blitz. (NARA)*

- Don't leave any fires burning. Damp them down, with salt if necessary.
- Atkinson advised against avoiding locking the doors of the house, likely because a locked door would hinder access by the fire and rescue services. She advises instead to leave the house unlocked, or to lock the house but pin up instructions about where the keys can be found.
- Wrap up warm – remember that the temperature will get colder throughout the night.

What you should take with you to a shelter

- The following important documents: identity card, rent book, building society book, record of instalment payments, ration card.
- Gas mask.
- Shaded torch.
- In cold weather, a hot-water bottle or oven-heated bricks 'wrapped up in your rugs or bedding to keep them warm'.
- Slippers and clean stockings or socks.
- Something to do (knitting etc.), something to read.
- 'Toilet soap, towel, toilet paper, something to drink out of, if you use a public shelter.'

While you are in the shelter

- Respect the Shelter Warden and comply with their orders and requirements.
- Assist the Shelter Warden practically if possible, and find other ways to contribute to shelter life, such as helping provide refreshments.
- Do your bit to promote morale within the shelter.

Your bed

- Atkinson explains that the best form of shelter bedding is a sleeping bag. She provides instructions about how to make one using a large (7ft × 6ft 6in) blanket, folded in two and sewn into a sleeping bag configuration, with reinforcing strips of fabric at the corners and along the edges.
- The sleeping bag needs to be ironed 'inside and out' at least once a month to maintain its freshness. All other bedding should also be ironed regularly, aired daily and if washable, laundered once a week.
- 'If you are allowed to leave your bedding in the shelter [. . .] leave it neatly folded, laid out on the bunk, not rolled up. There will be more chance of air penetrating through it if it is laid out in this way than if it is rolled up.'
- If you use loose bedding (e.g. blankets, sheets) rather than a sleeping bag, consider making a 'sleeping tidy', a large piece of material with tapes on the corners to tie the sheet to the bunk frame. This will keep the bedding from slipping off during the sleeping hours, and will keep the bunk tidy during the day.
- Do not store your bedding with other people's, as this facilitates the spread of diseases.

Children

- Try to persuade mothers with children to send their children away to the country. 'The best public shelter in the world is no place for children.'

▼ *A famous image of three London children, sitting with a strange mix of vulnerability and resilience outside a bombed-out home. (NARA)*

KEEPING WARM AND COMFORTABLE IN YOUR SHELTER

. . . and the help that is ready if your home is hit

If you are sleeping in an Anderson or brick surface shelter, every extra bit of immediate comfort and convenience that you can arrange in your shelter makes it easier for you to stand up to the bombing. Here are some hints taken from leaflets which are being issued to all shelterers by local authorities.

The Early Evening

For reading or knitting, a good lamp is necessary. Try a candle-lamp or nightlights. These are good for the eyes. Oil lamps are dangerous, as they may be spilled by shock from bombs. They make the air foul, too. If you do use one, be sure to put it out before going to sleep.

Heating

Never have a coke or other brazier in the shelter. They give off dangerous fumes. Oil stoves are also a source of danger, as they use up the oxygen which you need for breathing. A candle heater is useful. Put the candle in a flowerpot and then put a second flowerpot over the top. Raise the lower pot slightly from the ground. Try a hot water bottle or a hot brick in the bed. Heat the brick in the oven for two hours first and wrap it up.

Getting to sleep

A warm drink helps, particularly with children. Remember that when you are not sleeping on a thick mattress you need as much underneath you as on top. Have a good thick layer of newspapers or brown paper to lie on. Paper is draught proof. It is most important that bedding should be thoroughly aired every day.

In the night

Have something to eat, such as sweets or biscuits. Keep plenty of warm outdoor clothes beside you, in case you have to go out of the shelter. If you feel a draught, hang a curtain in front of the bunk. Wear ear plugs.

- Ensure that children are respectful and mindful of others in the shelter; especially, they should avoid running around and trampling on other people or their belongings.
- Arrange small, quiet play groups of multiple children. This will allow some mothers to get a little rest while you are keeping the children occupied.
- Before heading to the shelter, children should put on night clothes beneath their day clothes. This prevents keeping children in the same clothes day and night, and also, by removing their outer clothes, prevents them overheating in bed while they sleep.
- Atkinson reflected on the fact that 'ordinary rules for the care of children are now more important than ever'. She recommended 10–15 minutes of rest before and after meals; plenty of fresh air during the day; regular meals; 'plenty of milk'; nothing 'indigestible' or heavy to eat just before bedtime.
- Within a shelter, the children should be encouraged to say bedtime prayers. She adds rather poignantly: 'A child gains a great sense of security if it feels that someone is caring for it who is even greater than Mummy or Daddy.'
- If your child is under 10 years of age, ensure that it wears a label with its name and address written on. Also, teach all children to memorise their name and address as soon as they are able.
- Teach children 'not to touch anything strange which they find lying in the street or garden after an air raid'.

◀ *This very candid image of a tube station during the Blitz illustrates the close proximity of shelterers to the active Underground trains. (AirSeaLand Photos)*

ANIMALS IN THE BLITZ

Children were not the only vulnerable creatures facing the Blitz. There were also many issues surrounding what to do with animals, both pets and livestock. On the approach to war in the summer of 1939, there was mounting concern about what to do with domestic animals in the case of a strategic bombing campaign against Britain. The concern was on several fronts:

1. Domestic animals would be particularly exposed to the effects of bombing and gas attacks, as there would be no space allocated to them in shelters.
2. Pets would place a further drain on Britain's logistics, and there was no ration allocation for animals.
3. The need to look after pets might result in their owners making unwise decisions, e.g. staying in their home during an air raid to look after their pet.

In response to these concerns, the National Air Raid Precautions Animals Committee (NARPAC) was formed in 1939, and it published a notice to all pet owners entitled *Advice to Animal Owners*. One piece of its guidance was especially blunt: 'If at all possible, send or take your household animals into the country in advance of an emergency. […] If you cannot place them in the care of neighbours, it really is kindest to have them destroyed.' The anxiety brought about by the onset of war on 3 September 1939 meant that this advice was taken very literally. In fact, in the first week of the war it is estimated that a total of 750,000 dogs and cats were killed, most of the euthanasia performed by traumatised officers of the Royal Society for the Prevention of Cruelty to Animals (RSPCA), despite the fact that the RSPCA and many other animal charities opposed the measure.

As events later unfolded, it became evident that most of the animal executions were unnecessary, especially in areas that would remain largely untouched by war. Nevertheless, pet ownership did bring with it some problems. In the worst-hit areas, thousands of dogs and cats were left alone in rooms overnight, their owners fretful at the animal's state of mind or welfare. Feeding the animals, because of rationing, was also problematic, although most pet owners did seem to find just enough to keep their animals from starvation. Butchers, for example, would often have supplies of horse meat that could be purchased to feed to animals.

Looking beyond domestic pets, livestock obviously had an entirely different status, especially as government schemes actively encouraged people to keep chickens and pigs to help relieve some of the pressure on the official rationing system. Horses also still played an important logistical role, including within the Civil Defence organisations, the animals towing various pieces of equipment without using up precious fuel supplies.

The chief government publication relating to the care for animals during the war was the Home Office's *Air Raid Precautions for Animals* (1939). In a reflection of the lack of sentimentality inside the publication, the inside front cover featured a full-page advertisement for the '"Cash" Captive Bolt Pistol', which provided 'the speediest, most efficient and reliable means of destroying *any* animal, including horses, cats, and all sizes of dogs.' The booklet contained a full appendix on how to use this fatal instrument.

In terms of animals in urban areas, the advice was quite simple: have the creature evacuated or euthanised. Evacuation was not entirely impractical. The animals might be sent to relatives, but there were also several charitable organisations or wealthy private individuals who set up

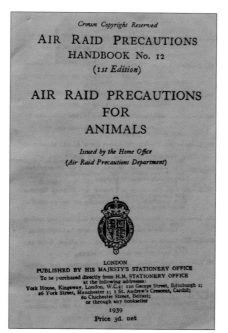

Crown Copyright Reserved

AIR RAID PRECAUTIONS
HANDBOOK No. 12
(1st Edition)

AIR RAID PRECAUTIONS
FOR
ANIMALS

Issued by the Home Office
(Air Raid Precautions Department)

LONDON
PUBLISHED BY HIS MAJESTY'S STATIONERY OFFICE
To be purchased directly from H.M. STATIONERY OFFICE
at the following addresses;
York House, Kingsway, London, W.C.2; 120 George Street, Edinburgh 2;
26 York Street, Manchester 1; 1 St. Andrew's Crescent, Cardiff;
80 Chichester Street, Belfast;
or through any bookseller
1939
Price 3d. net

sanctuaries for animals. (The famous Battersea Dogs' Home, established in 1860, looked after 145,000 dogs during the war, despite its precarious location in London.) Much of the book, however, was devoted to the protection and treatment of horses during air raids. It was recommended that stables be reinforced with sandbags or boxes filled with earth, to protect the creatures against flying splinters. It was important to keep fodder and water free from air raid contaminants, hence it was advised to keep them covered when not used, and aired for a few hours before consumption. This advice mainly applied to gas attacks, however, so was not relevant in the reality of the Blitz.

If horses were in the street during an air raid, it was advised to lead them into a side street or open area (the horse should not be ridden), unyoke them, and tie them up. For working horses that couldn't be relieved from their duties, 'A halter should be provided with a long lead which will enable the driver to maintain control of his animal while he is engaged in unyoking it. It may also be desirable, in order to assist control, to give a nose-bag feed or in some cases to cover the horse's head so as to obscure vision.' Practical stuff, but the 1939 manual also contains some advice that modern veterinary practice might find questionable, such as 'Small animals affected with shock should be kept quiet and warmly clothed; brandy, whisky, or sal volatile in small doses will afford temporary relief.'

AFTER THE RAID

What happened in the aftermath of a bombing raid was a matter of some contention in the UK in 1940 particularly. While the numbers of casualties caused by the bombing were thankfully overpredicted, the sheer administrative chaos of having to assist tens of thousands of homeless or displaced people was overwhelming.

The theory was far cleaner than the practice. For those coping with the immediate aftermath of housing loss, they could go to Rest Centres for instant respite and some food and drink. At the Rest Centre there would also be an officer (often someone with a legal background) responsible for giving out information about what to do next, particularly how to get essentials: money, clothing, a new ration book. Many of the physical objects required might be supplied by various charitable organisations, which did truly sterling work

◀ *Fuel was in rationed supply from 8 September 1939. Each petrol ration coupon was typically worth a gallon of fuel. (Author/1940s Swansea Bay)*

▼ *Following an air raid, some London chefs demonstrate the spirit of 'business as usual', an attitude much celebrated in the British press. (AirSeaLand Photos)*

throughout the Blitz, but for rehoming or the replacement of large volumes of furniture, the individuals would have to go to the local Assistance Board office, where they could apply for direct financial help.

This process is outlined in rough in an appropriately entitled booklet called *After the Raid*, published by the Ministry of Home Security in December 1940, during the height of the Blitz. In one passage it examples some of the financial and procedural rules:

Furniture and belongings

1. *If your income is below a certain amount* you can apply to the Assistance Board for:–
   (a) a grant to replace *essential* furniture and *essential* household articles;
   (b) a grant to replace your clothes or those of your family;
   (c) a grant to replace *tools* essential to your work.
   You also have a claim for your other belongings, but these do not come under the Assistance Board's scheme, and you should make your claims on Form V.O.W.1.
2. *If your income is above certain limits* you do not come under the Assistance Board's scheme and should make out a claim for all your belongings on Form V.O.W.1. The time at which payment can be made for belongings not covered by the Assistance Board's scheme will be settled shortly when Parliament has passed the War Damage Bill.

COMPENSATION FOR DAMAGE TO HOUSES
If you *own your house* or hold it on a long lease and it is damaged or destroyed, whatever your income, you should, as soon as possible, make a claim on Form W.O.W.1. The amount of your compensation and the time of paying it will depend on the passage of the War Damage Bill now before Parliament.

REPAIRS
If your house can be made fit to live in with a few simple repairs the local authority (apply to the Borough or Council Engineer) will put it right if the landlord is not able to do it. But how quickly the local authority can do this depends on local conditions.

In reality, this process could force traumatised people, often standing in the clothes that were now their only possessions, through a nightmare of bureaucratic dead ends and alleyways. One of the major problems was that the Assistance Boards were run by local authorities, but the displacement of war meant that literally hundreds of thousands of people shifted from one authority to another, with all the problems of record keeping, financial allocations and workload that entailed. It would take many months into 1941 before the system was working satisfactorily.

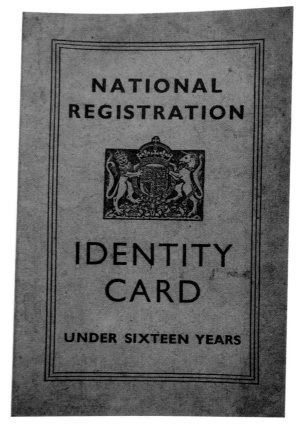

▲ *Identity cards were compulsory following the National Registration Act 1939. The scheme helped measures such as evacuation and rationing. (Author/1940s Swansea Bay)*

▼ *A ration book from the late war period. Typical weekly rations per adult included a single egg, 4oz of bacon/ham and 2oz of butter. (Author/1940s Swansea Bay)*

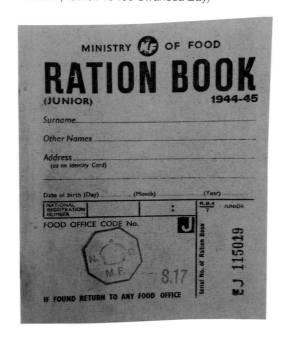

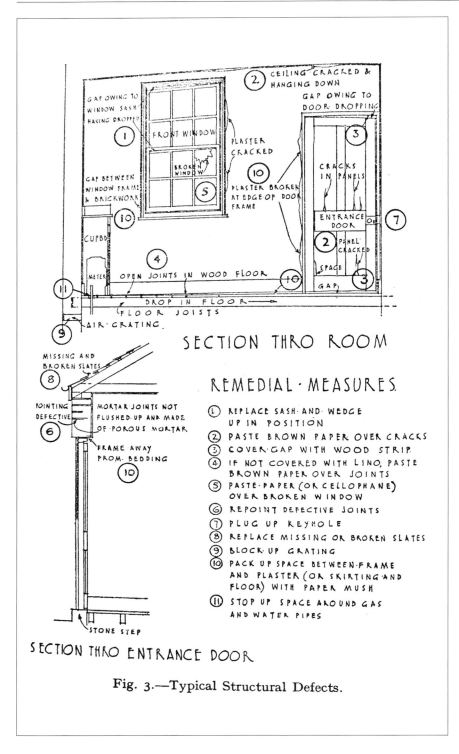

Fig. 3.—Typical Structural Defects.

◀ *A government booklet lists some of the structural defects that could affect homes following a bombing raid, and crude stop-gap 'remedial measures'. (Author/Joseph's Militaria)*

▼ *Government posters advising the British public how to identify various types of gas – here specifically Lewisite and mustard gas, both causing respiratory damage. (Author)*

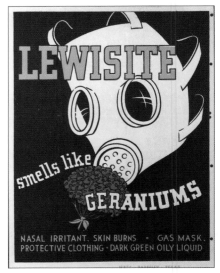

The Blitz was an astonishing event in human history. From one perspective, it was irredeemably bleak and horrific – no amount of cheery frontline humour can take away from the ghastly results of high explosive and incendiaries on the human body, and on the lives and property on which they fell. Yet we can acknowledge that under the most extreme pressures, ones that seem almost unfathomable in comfortable modern times, British society did not collapse, but kept trudging on, enduring. The motivational phrase 'Keep Calm and Carry On', developed by the Ministry of Information in 1939, has arguably been somewhat cheapened by its adaptation to modern marketing purposes. But at the time, it was something of a stoic masterpiece. It basically gave a message that would be absolutely relevant to the lives of those under German bombing: 'Don't panic, do the next thing in front of you, and you will get through.'

▼ *A shocked women, wheeling a few possessions from her bombed-out home, consults an ARP Warden about what to do next. Her first port of call would likely be a rest centre. (Shutterstock)*

BIBLIOGRAPHY AND FURTHER READING

PRIMARY SOURCES

Home Office (printed/published by HM Stationery Office):

Air Raid Precautions in Factories and Business Premises, Air Raid Precautions Handbook No. 6, 2nd edition (1936)

The Protection of your Home Against Air Raids (1938)

Personal Protection Against Gas, Air Raid Precautions Handbook No. 1, 2nd edition (1938)

Local Communications and Reporting of Air Raid Damage, Air Raid Precautions Memorandum No. 6, 1st edition (1938)

Personnel Requirements for Air Raid General and Fire Precautions Services and the Police Services, Air Raid Precautions Memorandum No. 7, 1st edition (1938)

The Duties of an Air Raid Warden, Air Raid Precautions Handbook No. 8, 2nd edition (1938)

Directions for the Erection and Sinking of the Galvanised Corrugated Steel Shelter (February 1939)

Rescue Parties and the Clearance of Debris, Air Raid Precautions Memorandum No. 2, 3rd edition (1939)

Organisation of the Air Raid Warden's Service, Air Raid Precautions Memorandum No. 4, 2nd edition (1939)

Incendiary Bombs and Fire Precautions, Air Raid Precautions Handbook No. 9, 1st edition (1939)

Air Raid Precautions for Animals, Air Raid Precautions Handbook No. 12, 1st edition (1939)

MINISTRY OF HOME SECURITY
(printed/published by HM Stationery Office):

Your Home as an Air Raid Shelter (1940)

Basic Training in Air Raid Precautions Air, Raid Precautions Training Manual No. 1, 1st edition (1940).

After the Raid (1940)

A.R.P. at Home: Hints for Housewives, by Mrs Creswick Atkinson (1941)

Rescue Service Manual, Air Raid Precautions Training Manual No. 3, 1st edition (1942)

The Fire Guards Handbook, Air Raid Precautions Handbook No. 14, 1st edition (1942)

Training in First Aid for Civil Defence Purposes, Air Raid Precautions Handbook No. 10, 2nd edition (1942)

OTHER:

Air Ministry, *Air Defence of Great Britain: Instructions for Observer Posts* (London, Air Ministry, 1941)

City of Sheffield Civil Defence, 'List of Public Air Raid Shelters at 6th September 1940 & General Information' (1940)

Haldane, J.B.S, *A.R.P.* (London, Victor Gollancz Ltd, 1938)

HM Government, Civil Defence Act 1939

Lord Privy Seal's Office, 'Your Food in Wartime' (July 1939)

Lord Privy Seal's Office, 'Evacuation: Why and How?' (July 1939)

Lord Privy Seal's Office, 'Fire Precautions in Wartime' (August 1939)

Mackenzie, R.J., *A.R.P.: Incendiary Bombs and How to Deal with Them*, Household Series Booklet No. 3 (Ottawa, Canada, Civil Air Raid Precautions, 1940)

Mackenzie, R.J., *A.R.P.: Make Your Home Your Air Raid Shelter*, Household Series Booklet No. 3 (Ottawa, Canada, Civil Air Raid Precautions, 1940)

Ministry of Home Protection, *Air Raids: What you must know, what you must do!* (London, HMSO, 1941)

National A.R.P. Animals Committee, 'Wartime Aids for All Animal Owners' (London, National A.R.P. Animals Committee/Home Office, 1939)

Thomas, S. Evelyn, *ARP: A Concise, Fully Illustrated and Practical Guide for the Householder and Air-Raid Warden*, 4th edition (London, Simpkin Marshall Ltd, 1939)

War Office, *Bomb Reconnaissance and Protection Against Unexploded Bombs* (London, War Office, August 1941)

SELECT SECONDARY SOURCES

Brayley, Martin J., *The British Home Front 1939–45* (Oxford, Osprey, 2005)

Brown, Mike, *Put that Light Out! Britain Civil Defence Services at War 1939–1945* (Stroud, Sutton Publishing, 1999)

Brown, Mike, *Wartime Britain* (Oxford, Shire, 2011)

Calder, Angus, *The Myth of the Blitz* (London, Pimlico, 1992)

Doyle, Peter, *ARP and Civil Defence in the Second World War* (Oxford, Shire, 2010)

Gardiner, Juliet, *Wartime Britain 1939–45* (London, Headline, 2005)

Gardiner, Juliet, *The Children's War* (London, Portrait, 2005)

Gardiner, Juliet, *The Blitz: The British Under Attack* (London, HarperPress, 2010)

Lowry, Bernard, *Britain's Home Defences* (Oxford, Osprey, 2004)

Price, Alfred, *Britain's Air Defences 1939–45* (Oxford, Osprey, 2004)

Ziegler, Philip, *London at War 1939–45* (London, Sinclair-Stevenson, 1992)

◀ *9th May 1945, St Paul's cathedral floodlit during victory celebrations in London at the end of the war in Europe. (Getty)*

INDEX

Page numbers in *italics* indicate illustration captions.